HOME SOLAR GARDENING

HOME SOLAR GARDENING

John H. Pierce

KEY PORTER BOOKS

To my grandmother Bessie Hewett — she grew her own supermarket and drugstore in the backyard

---

CANADIAN CATALOGUING IN PUBLICATION DATA

Pierce, John H., 1912-
Home solar gardening

Rev. ed.
Includes bibliographical references.
ISBN 1-55013-381-0

1. Solar greenhouses — Design and construction.
2. Greenhouse gardening. I. Title

SB415.P54 1992 690'.89 C91-095427-5

Key Porter Books Limited
70 The Esplanade
Toronto, Ontario
M5E 1R2

Printed and bound in Canada

Distributed in the United States of America by:

Publishers Group West
4065 Hollis
Emeryville, CA 94608

92 93 94 95 96 5 4 3 2 1

Contents

PREFACE

FIFTY YEARS AGO I built my first home greenhouse because I enjoyed the taste of fresh vegetables in the winter. About ten years ago there was a surge of interest in home greenhouses, and I designed one that is now on display at Longwood Gardens near Philadelphia. At that time I conducted well-attended workshops on the home solar greenhouse.

Now it seems that everyone is becoming environmentally aware. They are anxious to conserve energy and want to know how to proceed. This book is about one of the simplest things you can do—add a solar heat trap, called a solarium, greenhouse or solar grower, to your house. I like to grow winter salad greens in mine. You might want a hot tub in yours, or a combination of the two!

A solar greenhouse traps heat the same way that your car does when you park it in the sun. You can use this trapped solar energy to heat your greenhouse and reduce the cost of heating your residence. All it takes is a thermostatic fan that switches on automatically at a high temperature to blow heated air into the house. The Swansons in Waterdown, Ontario are only one example of many who have cut their heating cost by one-third by doing this, with strawberries in January as a bonus!

At present I do my solar growing in a curved-eave, double-glazed, acrylic structure which is under the shade of a maple tree all summer, and fully exposed to sun energy during the winter.

My hope is that this book will help you get started in saving heating costs and having fresh watercress salads all winter.

The text, data, resources and bibliography have all been brought up to date, so that you can use them with confidence. If you have any problems I would be glad to try to help you.

Every book represents the expertise and inspiration of many people. For sharing their solar secrets I am grateful to Dr. Paul Moses, Dow Chemical; Bryan Boardman, Boardman Electronics; Rick Tarrant, Nu-Age Manufacturing; Rob McCormack.

For contributing in various ways, a word of appreciation to Leib Wolofsky, Roland Barnsley, Herschel Swanson, Jim Cunning and Dorothea Schaab. To my very talented wife Marian, thanks for providing the life-support systems that make any book possible.

John H. Pierce
15008 Niagara Parkway
Niagara-on-the-Lake
Ontario, Canada
L0S 1J0

INTRODUCTION

LIFE ON EARTH existed long before man, supported by the energy of the sun. Common sense suggests that we have all the energy we need to do anything and everything, in the form of a nuclear fusion generator called the sun, installed an appropriate distance away by non-human intelligence. The instinctive wisdom of the gopher tells it to dig its burrow on a sunny slope facing the equator with a thin sod roof to absorb solar energy. Many of our ancestors were sun worshippers who knew instinctively that life was dependent upon the sun.

Primitive man considered the sun a god, and early civilizations, such as those in India, Egypt and Mexico, built temples to the sun. About 1200 B.C. the Babylonians used sun data to make one of the earliest calendars. The Greek Colossus of Rhodes was a 105 foot (32 m) tall statue of Apollo, the sun god. The Romans gave us the word "sol," which is a part of many of our sun terms. The Aztecs, Mayans and Incas considered the sun the source of all life, and in some cases even made human sacrifices to honor the sun. Many early cultures built their homes facing the sun to receive the warmth of winter solar energy. The Japanese flag with the rising sun emblem is a vestige of ancient oriental sun worship. Before we took our long detour into technological and industrial excess, we did many things with sun energy to make life fulfilling and pleasant. We are now coming out of this detour with a new realization that we can use sun energy to enrich our lives.

Today, we are in the midst of change. We are faced not only with change necessitated by energy problems, but also with a world-wide yearning for a better quality of life. One of the easy, inexpensive things that you can do at home to save energy and live better is solar gardening. Your solar grower may be a cloche or shed in the backyard, a window sill garden, plant room, sun porch, balcony box or a solar greenhouse, using sun energy for heat and growing. To make maximum use of sun energy requires an understanding of the principles involved, and a few simple techniques in construction or adaptation. That's what this book is all about.

The next major household appliance may well be a solar grower, which will cost little or nothing to operate and which will probably add heat to the residence as well as provide food and flowers. Sure, you can put a solar collector on the roof and heat your water. But why do that when you can use a solar grower that acts as a collector to heat your water and that also gives you the bonus of strawberries in mid-winter? Better living begins with better food and you can control the nutritional quality of the food in your home solar grower. The solar grower means you can have the "green feeling" twelve months of the year. The snow may be deep and the bitter wind howling, but the orchids are blooming and the tomatoes taste delicious!

A new energy awareness is motivating people all over the planet to experiment and devise the techniques we need to use solar energy at home. Most of the techniques are passive, using only the energy of the sun in very simple ways. Innovators are not waiting for engineers, scientists, governments or universities to develop large-scale active systems, which use sun energy plus electrical energy to run pumps, blowers, motors and controls in expensive, complex arrangements. You can profit by sharing experiences with solar innovators everywhere, and in the Resource List at the end of this book you will find information to help you get in touch with your fellow solar adventurers. I would be glad to hear from you and share solar experiences.

As we develop more solar expertise we will be able to defy seasonal change and store the heat of summer for winter use. Already we have a few homes doing this with very expensive and elaborate equipment. No doubt the future will see new techniques for collection and practical hold-over heat systems for the average home-owner. After all, we are now operating on hold-over energy stored in fossil fuels, so the hold-over principle comes straight from nature and contemporary technology.

The highest intensity of sunlight in the solar system is found not on the surface of the sun, but on the roof of the University of Chicago Physics Laboratory using the new "light funnel," or nonimaging light concentrator. The Illinois Department of Agriculture in Springfield uses 12,000 square feet of these collectors to heat and cool the building. Southern California Edison now has eight solar power plants that generate electricity for 385,000 people, and predicts that their cheapest source of electricity will be solar within five years. We are rapidly moving into the solar age. Out of the bewildering array of solar developments, there are things you can do at home now. All kinds of people are interested and would like to do something about solar energy, but they don't know where to begin. This book will help you get started.

The following terms are used in *Home Solar Gardening*. *Solar gardening* is the art of using the light and heat energy of the sun to grow plants. A *solar grower* is a special structure, or modification of an existing structure, that permits you to extend the growing season or to grow plants right through the winter, using sun energy. A *passive solar system* is one using only the energy of the sun. An *active solar system* is one which uses additional sources, such as electricity, to power equipment of various kinds. In most climates, you can grow a wide range of plants with a passive solar grower. In the colder climates, or to grow some tropical plants, you may have to use an active system with a back-up heat source. What makes the solar grower different from the old conventional greenhouse is the use of insulation, reflective materials, improved glazing and heat storage devices.

Following are some of the solar growers considered in this book:

- *Cloches* are small portable covers usually used to extend the season.
- *Frames* and *boxes* are low, permanent structures, also used to extend the normal growing season.
- The *attached solar grower* is a walk-in structure with access to the house.
- The *free-standing solar grower* is much like a standard greenhouse with the modification mentioned above.
- The *solar sun* pit is dug into the ground to conserve heat.

Figure 1. A home-built solar grower.

Chapter 1

MAKING USE OF THE SUN

THERE ARE a number of reasons for having your own solar grower, and the solar techniques involved in operating a solar grower are relatively simple. We are already making use of stored solar energy in the form of fossil fuels and wood and hydroelectric power, which depends on the power of the sun to operate the water cycle. Solar energy makes possible evaporation of water from the earth to the clouds. When it comes back as rain to fill the rivers, we harness it to produce electricity. Using solar energy is not as foreign or strange as you may think.

Why Have a Solar Grower?

TO SAVE MONEY

You can have a solar grower in your home with no addition to your heating bill. In fact, if the grower is well engineered you can add heat to your residence. Considering the price of food and the cost of fuel you use when shopping, you really can save money. Many families report savings of $200 to $500 just on the cost of vegetables. You can grow cut flowers and potted plants for the house for only the cost of a packet of seed.

In addition to the savings on food and flowers, you can save by growing your own bedding plants, as well as trees and shrubs for the yard. Few of us have as many colorful bedding plants as we would like, often because our budgets will not permit it. Growing your own plants places no limit on the quantity you can grow. I have grown 5,000 perennials in a 16 foot square (24 m^2) solar grower in one season. Seed costs are minimal and, with solar energy for heat production, total costs are low. You may consider this process too slow for trees and shrubs that you want to use for home landscaping, but you'd be surprised how rapidly rooted cuttings and seedlings turn into mature plants. I have in my yard a Princess or Karri tree, *Paulownia tomentosa*, that is 14 feet (4 m) tall and only three years old. I grew the tree from seed started in my solar grower. Not all plants grow this rapidly, but this tree illustrates the fact that you can grow your own landscape material in a reasonable length of time and at little cost.

Until she married a botanist, my wife had never enjoyed a whole spray of *Cymbidium* orchids in the living room. I couldn't afford to buy even one spray, but now I can grow many.

One of my friends, a retired electronics engineer, built an eave-to-ground solar grower on the side of his house facing the equator (Figure 1) and lowered his fuel consumption from 900 gallons (4100 l) of oil per year to 250 gallons (1100 l). With the cost of oil steadily increasing, this represents a substantial saving. Not only that, my friend enjoyed fresh strawberries in the middle of winter. That's not bad for Canada north of Toronto.

I have talked with many people living in very cold climates who report little or no cost to heat a solar grower. Although solar growers often use the heating system of the residence extended into the grower, the owners find that there is no increase in overall heating costs to grow plants all winter.

TO SAVE ENERGY

We now have, in almost every kitchen, appliances such as deep-freezers, refrigerators and stoves. A solar grower means less use of the freezer and refrigerator because you grow your own fresh vegetables all year round. Fresh salads probably mean less cooking. Thus, the solar grower may well save, rather than use, energy. Consider what it costs to grow, harvest, pack, store, ship and display a head of lettuce. Compare this with the cost of walking to your own solar grower, and picking and washing lettuce for the table. The energy savings of growing your own vegetables can be enormous!

FOR FRESHNESS, QUALITY AND VARIETY

I am sure that you have gone into the produce section of some stores and found limp, flaccid lettuce. You have no way of knowing how long it has been since the lettuce was picked, or where it has been, but you can be certain that the longer the time from harvest to table, the more the lettuce will deteriorate. When you pick an apple or cut leaves of lettuce or stems of roses, you are removing the cut portion from its life-support system and changes begin to occur. Wilting happens first. There is no root system to supply fluids and keep pressure in the cut part. The tissues continue to metabolize after separation. Actually this is when the process of decomposition starts. Natural flavor dissipates or dramatically changes, the vitamin content decreases or disappears and there is a decline in the amount of sugar retained in the tissues.

You have probably observed how an apple left out at room temperature shrivels and dries out. This is a good example of what happens to all plant tissue cut from the growing plant. Proper home preservation methods such as canning, freezing and drying will give you high quality foods, but they will not equal fresh foods. The best-tasting and the highest quality food still comes from practising harvest to table the same day. And that you can do in your home solar grower.

When you confine your food intake to what you find in stores, you are limited to what someone else chooses to grow. In your own solar grower, you can produce the host of odd and unusual vegetables and herbs that make dining a delightfully varied experience. You can inject a new spirit of creativity into your cooking.

FOR BETTER NUTRITION

At least some of the produce that you buy is grown more for appearance and shipping qualities than for nutritional content. In your home solar grower, you can build good nutrition into your food and forget other considerations.

Start with a garden fertilizer which has about equal amounts of nitrogen, phosphate and potash. As a rule of thumb, nitrogen goes to green foliage, phosphates to flower and fruit and potash to general sturdiness of the whole plant. But don't stop there! Plants need other things in order to be top quality human food, and you can get them all by feeding the plants something from the sea, or compost, or both.

Most of the minor or micro nutrients, minerals and organic compounds that are present on land eventually end up in the sea. Rains fall and leach these ingredients out of the soil into our rivers and finally into the ocean. Many of the earlier peoples buried fish under the hills of maize. You can do the same thing more conveniently by using a seaweed or fish fertilizer. If you use a fish fertilizer, make sure that it is 100 percent fish emulsion. In many places the processor simply takes whole herring and grinds it to form a sticky, thick liquid emulsion. Liquefied fish will improve flavor and nutritional quality in food grown hydroponically or in soil. Very small quantities added to a water solution are sufficient for good growth.

FOR SELF-CARE

Long before there was a corner drugstore, medicine came from practical botany. People have always used plants or plant products to treat various ailments and to improve health.

Plants manufacture not only carbohydrates, sugars and proteins, but also many other compounds such as oils, fats, waxes, resins, perfumes and alkaloids or drugs. Among these are many substances that we use for self-care, and they can easily be grown in your home solar grower. Every day for nearly a year, I walked through the greenhouse, cut a small slice of *Aloe vera* leaf and rubbed the juices on the back of my hand. Eventually, the age spots faded and disappeared. *Aloe vera* has been extensively used for the treatment of X-ray burns. Application of the juice to burns promotes healing without any noticeable scar tissue.

Only a few years ago, the drugstore had only a limited selection of soaps. Recently I counted fourteen varieties for sale made from such ingredients as cucumber, strawberry, sunflower, violet and a host of other plant substances. Making your own soap from plants grown in your own solar grower is much easier than you think, and as with food, you have control over the ingredients. You can forget the many problems traceable to additives.

The range of useful ingredients for self-care products that you can grow is extensive. Such things as astringents, bath and body lotions, breath sweeteners, deodorants, facial packs, gargles, mouthwashes, ointments, shampoos, salves, tonics, teas and toothpastes are just a few examples. In Chapter 12, you'll find a list of these self-care products and the plants from which they are derived. You may not save a lot of money growing your own self-care products, but you will get high quality and purity.

FOR FRAGRANCE

When you walk into your solar grower in the middle of winter and catch the aroma of freesia, jasmine or sweet pea, it is exhilarating.

I think we overlook the health value of fresh fragrance. There is something about the aroma of fresh flowers that is soothing, tranquilizing and at the same time invigorating. I am certain that one reason we travel miles to the mountains and the tropics is a deep subliminal need for the refreshment of fragrance.

We use quantities of perfumes; some are from natural plant sources, but most are synthetic copies of plant aromas. We have forgotten many of the ways to use plant fragrance at home. Grandmother's house had sachets tucked into many of the bureau drawers and potpourris on the mantel or bathroom shelf. Many of these were made from roses, thyme, lavender, violets, rosemary, balsam fir and other common plants that are easy to grow in your solar grower.

Mention of the word *incense* may conjure up visions of heady dens of iniquity, but incense can also be refreshing. We seem to remember scents and they often bring back very pleasant experiences. This past Christmas I had a pine-scented candle on the mantel, and I sensed that the visitors were relaxing, perhaps remembering time spent in a pine forest. Whenever I have South African freesia blooming at home, people are intrigued by the unique, delicate fragrance. In the many species of eucalyptus from Australia, there is a wide range of aromas, and some of these plants do very well in the home solar garden.

Outdoors, in the natural setting, plants pass off in vapor, or volatilize, compounds into the air. A new field of botany called *allelopathy* studies the way in which these volatilized substances affect life forms, including the human race, My suspicion is that you could reduce the need for tranquilizers by growing plants for fragrance.

FOR THERAPY

A short while ago I had occasion to visit a home for the aged and was surprised to find that they had a greenhouse. When I asked the administrator about it, he told me that a few years ago the staff was concerned because the patients seemed listless and discontented. A nearby commercial grower donated a plant to each occupant. Caring for a single plant improved the dispositions of the occupants to such an extent that the institution built a greenhouse addition to the building. This same episode has been repeated all over the world and has established horticultural therapy as a recognized treatment. It feels good to do things with plants: when you come from work and go into your solar grower to see if the radishes are up or the cymbidiums in bloom, you get a lift of spirit, "the green feeling," an amazing antidote for stress. Perhaps this is because flowers have traditionally been a part of our rituals from wedding to funeral, solace to the ill, decoration for the church altar and a non-verbal love token from person to person. Perhaps it rouses ancient feelings of kinship with plants when we watch seeds germinate, cuttings take root and flowers open. Or maybe it is as simple as the summer picnic feeling in mid-winter, minus the ants! Without trying to understand it, you can feel it when you go into your solar grower to share in the life process with plants.

There may also be an atmospheric reason, known as negative ion air, for feeling better around plants. Molecules of air sometimes carry either a positive or negative electrical charge. You can probably recall the sensation of fresh exhilaration in the air right after a thunderstorm. This may be due to the fact that the earth is negative and the atmosphere positive so that when lightning strikes, it grounds the clouds, changing the air from an excess of positive ions to a surplus of negative ions. There is some evidence to show that you feel better when the air contains more negative than positive ions. Lightning, ocean surf and waterfalls all act as negative ion generators, and so do plants. In your solar grower, the plants are conducting the negative charge of the earth up to the leaves and out into the air as water vapor, oxygen and carbon dioxide. So, for a number of reasons it is evident that the feeling that greenery creates is beneficial to human health and peace of mind.

FOR FAMILY TOGETHERNESS

Solar growing at home is one of the few activities in which the entire family can participate. Children are fascinated by the life process when they germinate seed and proud when they eat radishes which they have grown. Retired persons find growing food and flowers a fulfilling hobby. For the gourmet cook, there is the satisfaction of fresh herbs and spices. For everyone there is the pleasure of fresh flowers on the table, grown in a special place that fosters sharing and reverence for life.

FOR CHEMICAL-FREE FOOD

There is really no way of knowing what chemicals have been applied to the food that you buy. Even in the countries with chemical restrictions, you may be eating food imported from another country with very lax laws relating to what is sprayed on food plants.

There are three types of chemicals which may be used on commercially grown food: pesticides, fungicides and weed killers. These chemicals are formulated to kill, or control, insects, diseases and troublesome weeds. It really doesn't make any sense for one life form, man, to ingest chemicals made to kill another life form. The trend in commercial food growing is away from using such hazardous chemicals and toward practising integrated pest management. This means that the grower maintains good sanitation, uses baits, traps and biological controls such as predators or organic substances known to be safe for human consumption. However, it is still difficult for the consumer to identify food grown in this way.

It is also very difficult to know which additives have been used to preserve or color the food you eat. There is a growing body of literature which indicates that many of the chemicals used as additives may be injurious to your health. The simple way to avoid both chemical sprays and additives is to grow your own food at home, in your solar grower.

Everywhere in the world, we are becoming more aware of our responsibility for planetary housekeeping. Whenever sprays are applied to growing things, some of the spray escapes into the environment and gets into the food chains, and we have contaminated fish, birds, animals and plants that may be part of our diet. Residues of many of these chemicals accumulate over long periods of time or become concentrated as they move up the food chains. All over the world, there is a quickening concern about releasing long-term toxins into our water systems. The next big shortage, after oil, may well be clean, healthful water. Home growing can help keep our water clean.

FOR STAY-AT-HOME TRAVEL

For a lot less than a trip to the tropics, you can stay home, sit under the bougainvillea, smell the jasmine and bask in the warm sunshine in your own solar grower. As the cost of energy rises higher and higher, stay-at-home travel becomes worth considering. What sometimes prompts travel is the desire for a new, fresh environment. Soft breezes, perfumed air and warm sunshine are restorative and refreshing. You can reproduce these conditions right at home with tropical plants in a solar grower or solarium and save a lot of money.

Using the Sun for Growth, Heat and Work

In your solar grower you are using light in at least three ways; for growth, for heat and to run equipment. In order to use your solar grower effectively you need to understand the differences in the three

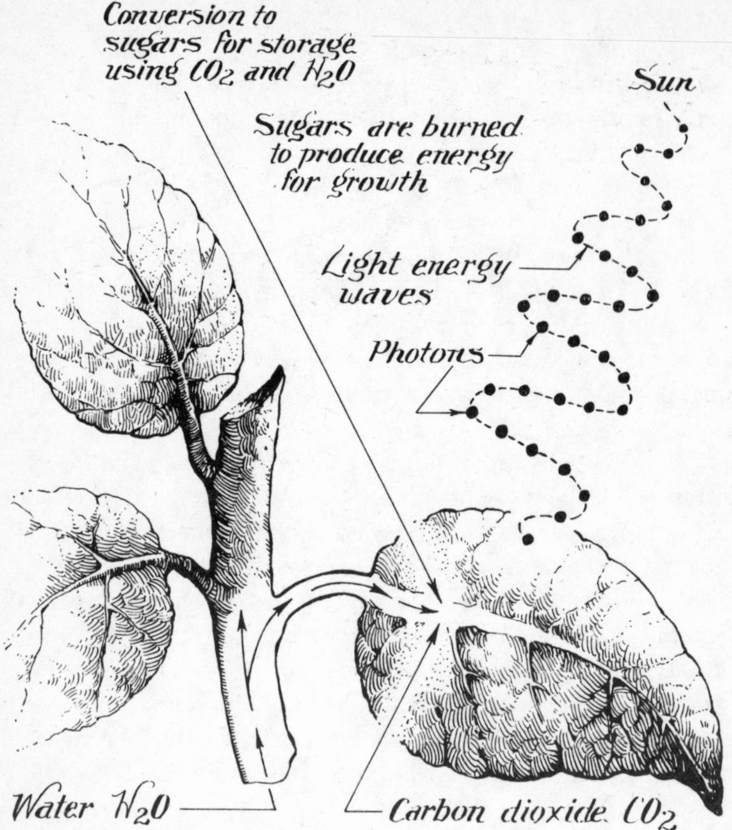

Figure 2. Light energy is used by plants for growth.

ways that you use light from the sun. We are used to thinking of light only as the visible part of the energy spectrum that comes from the sun.

Light travels from the sun as short-wave radiation. Plants use the visible spectrum as well as the invisible solar radiation for growth. The light travels as waves that are made up of little bits of energy called photons. When the photons strike the leaf they release energy. The plant leaf uses this energy to make sugars and starches which are stored. Then the plant uses this stored energy for growth. Thus, the more light that strikes the plants in your solar grower, the more energy you have for growth (Figure 2). When you buy bulbs or seed, for example, you are really buying stored energy. If the plants were well grown, with plenty of light, then your seed has ample energy for germination and your bulbs will produce large flowers.

Figure 3. A solar vent.

When light strikes objects, it turns to heat. So any solid object or material in the solar grower absorbs some heat. Obviously you will want to use the materials that absorb heat best. The sunlight comes through the covering of your solar grower as short waves. When the short-wave radiation strikes an object, it turns into long heat waves, some of which cannot go back out through the covering. This is a heat trap. How many times have you left a parked car to come back and find the seats so hot you couldn't sit on them? This is the principle involved in producing solar heat for your grower.

Light may also perform work when it strikes a device such as the solar vent (Figure 3). This is a thermal piston containing fluid that expands when heated and contracts as it cools. I use this to open and close ventilators and louvres automatically so that even when I am away there is no danger of overheating the solar grower. This device is especially useful in the small solar grower where temperatures can rise very rapidly.

Solar, or photovoltaic cells, have the unique capacity to convert sunlight into electricity, which you can then use to operate lights,

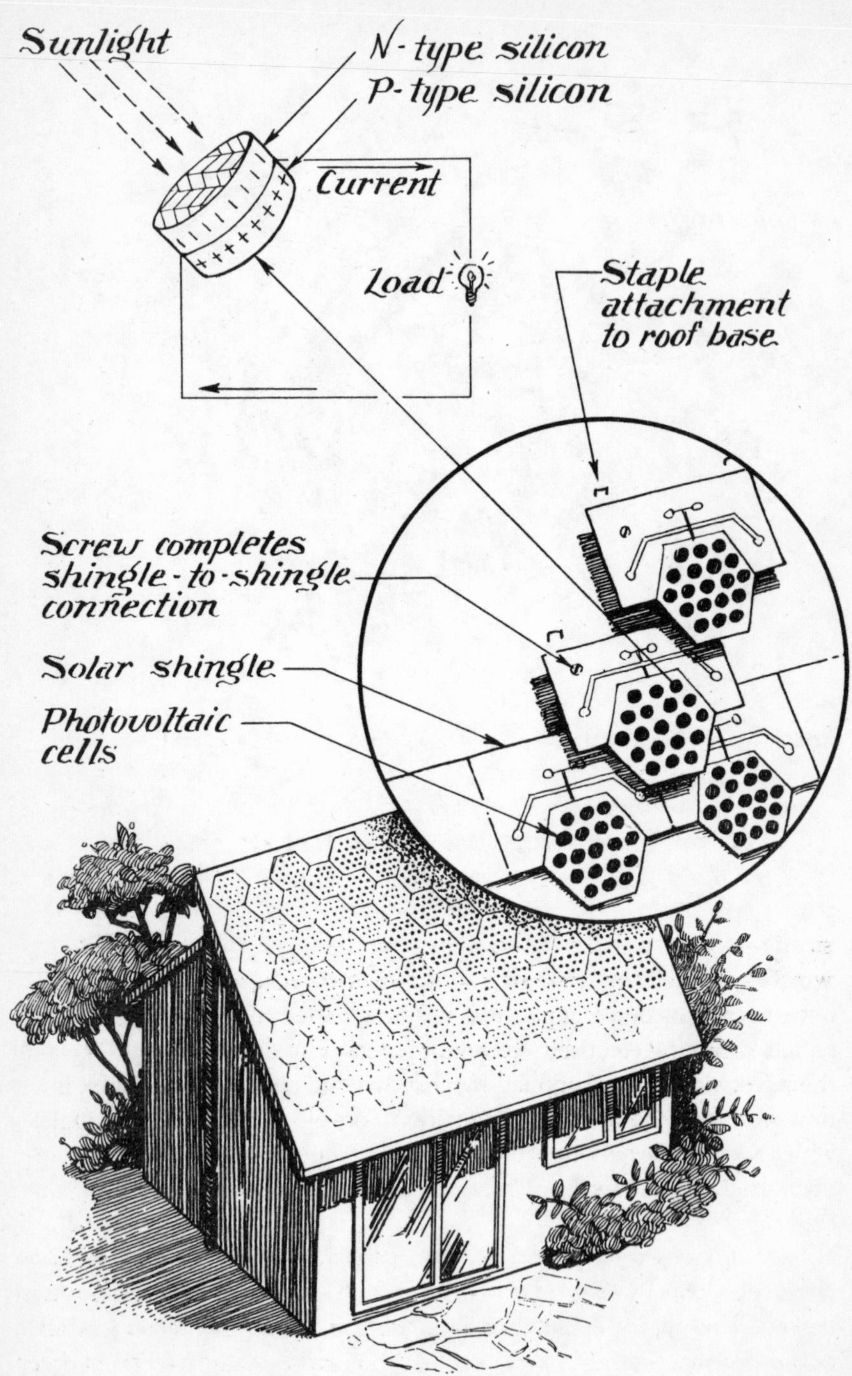

Figure 4. Photovoltaic cells in shingles.

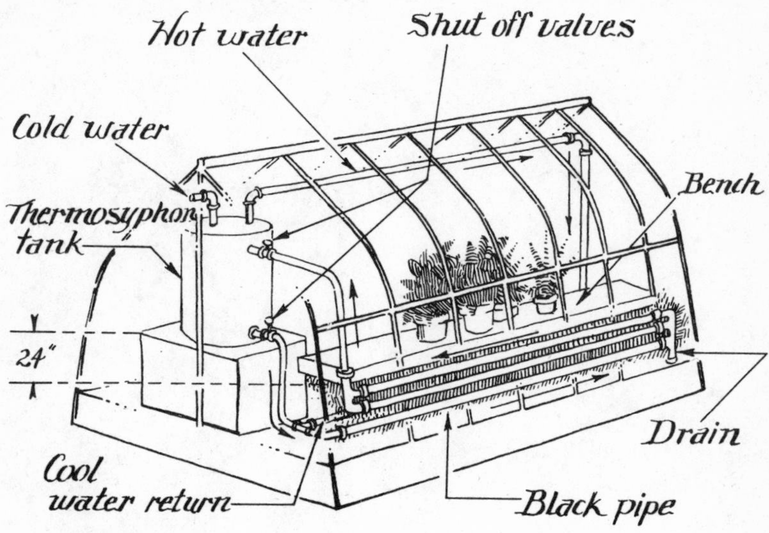

Figure 5. In a thermosyphon system, cold water enters the top of the tank, sinks to the bottom and moves to the black pipe collector by gravity. The water is heated in the collector and goes back to the top of the tank (hot water rises) and then into the solar grower.

small motors and heaters. You have doubtless seen solar cell calculator watches and lighting systems. Until recently larger photovoltaic panels have been considered expensive, but now there are thousands of these panels supplying electricity to remote areas. Hundreds of homes have all their electrical needs supplied by photovoltaic panels, and Solarex is now working with a roofing company to develop photovoltaic shingles which would do the same (Figure 4). There are many suppliers of complete photovoltaic systems and the cost keeps coming down every year (see Resources).

The thermosyphon is a device which collects sun heat in air or water and moves it by natural convection. Both air and water rise when heated. This means that you can use the thermosyphon, without other power, to circulate heated air or water through the solar grower. In order to operate, the thermosyphon collector must be below the solar grower, in the case of air, and below the storage tank for water (Figure 5).

Figure 6. A two-storey solar grower.

Chapter 2

BUILDING AN ATTACHED SOLAR GROWER

PERHAPS the most satisfactory type of solar grower is the structure with direct access to the house, which you design and build yourself. Adapting a prefabricated structure will be discussed in a later chapter. If you don't feel comfortable designing your own structure, have an architect or builder do it for you. It is important to plan the solar grower carefully and to make changes on paper, so that when you build you have everything the way you want it. Very often a professional design will save you money in the long run.

Advantages

There are several advantages to building your own solar grower, or having it built by a contractor to your specifications.

1. You can control the appearance of the structure and make certain that it blends well with the color and architecture of the house. The framing material may be the same as the siding on the residence. If the house is brick or stucco, then you can choose stained or painted wood to match.

2. You can locate a custom-made structure in places where a prefabricated unit might not fit. I am currently building such a solar grower. It is L-shaped to fit in a sunny corner facing the equator.

3. You can make the solar grower any size you wish. You can provide enough space to accommodate your family and their particular activities. For example, you may want a space for dining as well as enough bench and ground space to grow winter food for the family.

4. You can build the solar grower up to the eave of the house and have a two-storey structure with a balcony for dining and lounging and a wrought-iron spiral staircase down to the growing area.

5. You have complete freedom to use benches, staging, shelves, ground beds, hydroponics, planters and hanging baskets. Just as you express your creative talents in the decoration of the inside of the house, so you can create a unique sun garden in the solar grower.

Orientation

Face your solar grower toward the equator. If this is not possible, orient a separate collector toward the equator and transfer the heat into the solar grower. In some cases, the remote collector can be located on the roof of the house and provide enough heat for residential hot water as well as heat for the solar grower. Get a solar contractor for this type of collector. If you can't face the grower toward the equator and if there is no room for a remote collector, then the next best answer is to orient the structure to the east.

The Chill Factor

If you live in an area where there are cold winter winds, you will lose a lot of heat at night because of the effect of the chill factor. The following chart will show you how important the chill factor is on exposed human flesh and to a lesser extent on other surfaces.

If the wind is blowing across your solar grower at 20 miles (32 km) per hour and the temperature is 25°F (−4°C), then your heat losses are actually those for −4°F (−20°C). This suggests that if you have this kind of situation, you should consider evergreen windbreaks to divert, or cut down, the force of the wind.

CHILL FACTOR

		Wind in **miles per hour**/*km per hour*				
Temperature		**10**	**20**	**30**	**40**	**50**
°F	*°C*	*16*	*32*	*48*	*64*	*80*
35°	*2°*	21°	12°	5°	1°	0°
		−6°	*−11°*	*−15°*	*−17°*	*−18°*
30°	*−1°*	16°	3°	−2°	−4°	−7°
		−9°	*−16°*	*−19°*	*−20°*	*−22°*
25°	*−4°*	9°	−4°	−11°	−15°	−17°
		−13°	*−20°*	*−24°*	*−26°*	*−27°*
20°	*−7°*	2°	−9°	−18°	−22°	−24°
		−17°	*−23°*	*−28°*	*−30°*	*−31°*
10°	*−12°*	−9°	−24°	−33°	−36°	−38°
		−23°	*−31°*	*−36°*	*−38°*	*−39°*
0°	*−18°*	−22°	−40°	−49°	−54°	−56°
		−30°	*−40°*	*−45°*	*−48°*	*−49°*

Designing

Once you have located your solar grower and protected it from the wind, there are three things to remember that are important for the solar structure:

1. Get all the light and heat possible into the grower.
2. Put materials that will absorb heat inside the grower.
3. Use insulation to keep the heat in the grower as long as possible.

With these criteria in mind, here are some suggestions to help you design your own solar grower.

Foundations

The foundation for a solar grower is different from that for a greenhouse, because the foundation is a good place to put a large amount of heat storage material. The more heat storage material you can get into the floor and foundation, the more room you'll have inside the grower for plants.

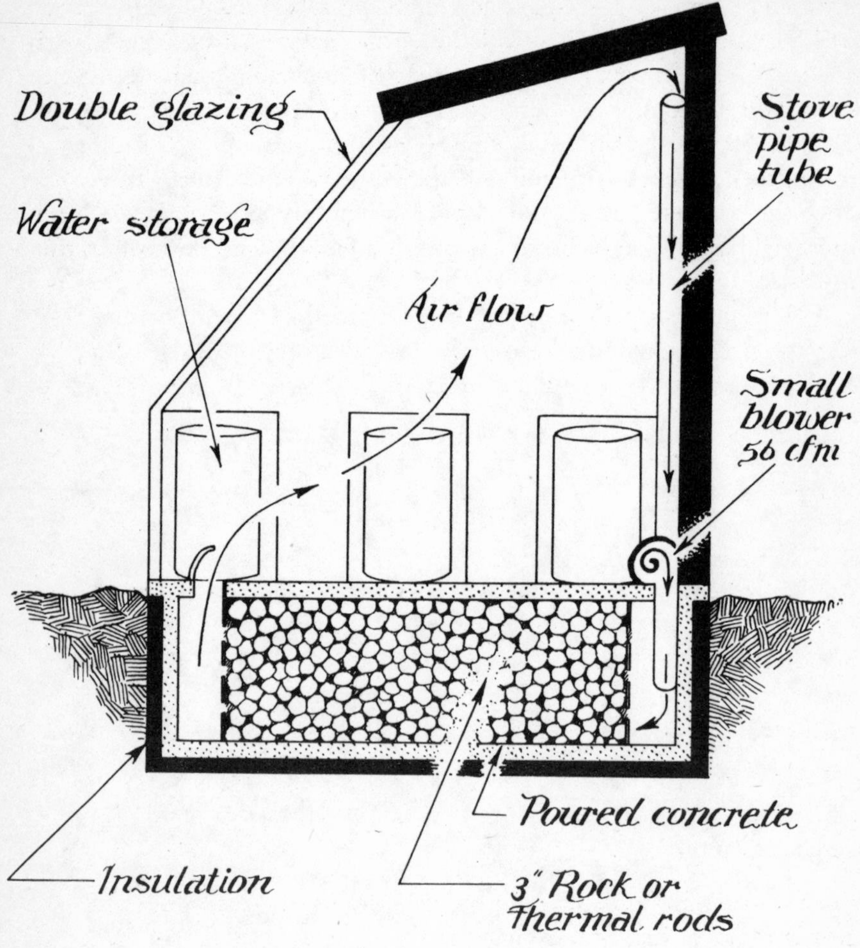

Figure 7. *An active solar grower.*

One of the best solutions to this situation is to excavate a hole the size of the grower to a depth of 18 inches (46 cm) or down to the frostline. Fill the hole with rocks to within 6 inches (15 cm) of the top. The rocks should be fist size or larger, although broken concrete will do. Next, mix concrete to pour into the hole full of rocks, using one part (by volume) of cement to two parts sand and six parts gravel. Add enough water to make a thin soupy mixture that flows easily. Pour this mix into the hole and the concrete will flow down through the stones to give you a solid slab 18 inches (46 cm) thick. If the mix doesn't go down between the rocks easily, add more water or tamp down the mix with a stick. When you have filled the hole, level off the concrete with a board. Before the concrete sets up, draw a line along each edge and set in bolts, head down, so that you can fasten the sill of the grower to the slab. If there are no rocks available on your property, you can buy pit-run rock from a quarry and save the cost of a solid cement base. Once the concrete has set, dig a trench around the edge of the slab and insert rigid insulation board to a depth of 2 feet (60 cm) or down to the frostline.

Insulation of all kinds is rated for resistance to the movement of heat through the material. This rating is called the R factor. I use a polyurethane board, faced with aluminum on both sides, that is rated at an R value of seven, for 1 inch (2.5 cm) of thickness. If you live in a very cold climate, I would use an insulation board with at least an R factor of ten. This type of foundation is a passive solar heat storage device which requires no additional equipment.

An alternative active heat storage system is shown in Figure 7. This system requires a standard poured concrete wall or block foundation with an insulated base. The rounded rock, 3 inches (7 cm) in diameter is loose in the base and a small blower circulates the warm air from the top of the grower down to the rock for storage. The floor is reinforced concrete with vent openings, so that at night the warm air rises to keep the grower well heated.

If you live in a climate zone where you don't need much heat storage, then you can use metal leg anchors on a wood base with no foundation. Even then, I would suggest you dig a trench around the perimeter and insulate. This permits the ground inside the solar grower to act as heat storage material.

Construction

The frame of the grower can be standard building construction using 2 by 4 or 2 by 6 lumber with two important exceptions:

1. The lumber used for the walls and the roof must be rabbeted, or grooved, to receive glass or other glazing material, as shown in Figure 8.

2. Construct the glazed surface, facing the equator, at an angle of your latitude plus ten degrees. This is the angle perpendicular to the rays of the winter sun position (Figure 9). The angle is not critical. If, for any reason, you want to change the angle by ten degrees, you

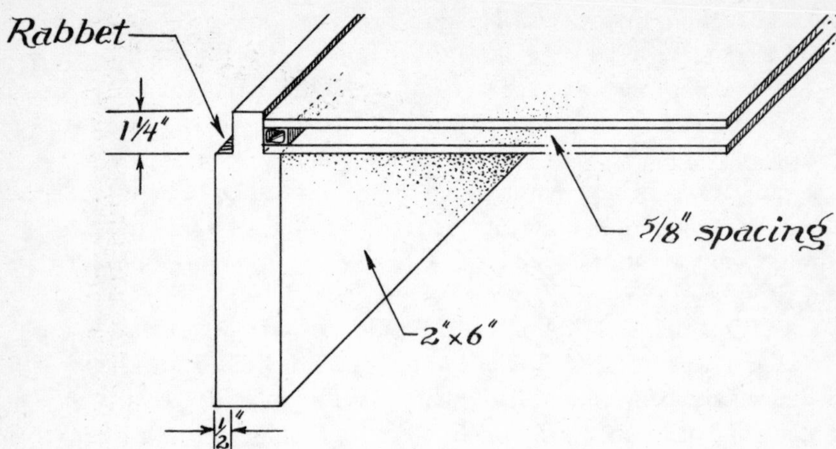

Figure 8. Rabbeting for glazing.

will still receive 98 percent of the optimum amount of light. The sun moves across the sky daily and shifts from north to south seasonally, so your solar grower collector seldom functions at maximum. A tracking collector which follows the sun is the only way to maintain perfect alignment with the solar rays.

Before you erect the frame on the base, make sure of a waterproof joint where the wood uprights meet the wall of the house. You can do this with closed-cell rubber or foam stripping, which will make a tight fit against almost any surface. Where the ridge meets the house, use flashing to prevent leaking.

One of the little things that makes a big difference is the width of the door. There are many times when it would be convenient to take a standard wheelbarrow through the doorway to take out rubbish or bring in fresh soil. You can make, or buy, a 36 inch (90 cm) door that matches the house and will give you wheelbarrow access.

Glazing

The term glazing refers to any type of transparent or translucent covering that you use on the solar grower. Your solar grower requires double glazing, as two layers of covering will reduce the heat loss by about 30 percent. I enjoy being able to watch the snow swirling about while I plant seeds for spring flowers, so let's consider the transparent glazing materials first.

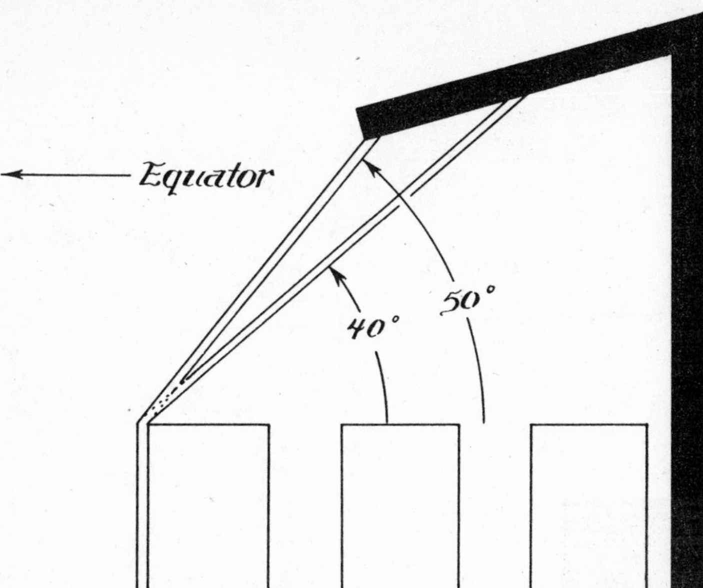

Figure 9. Glazing angle. At 40° latitude, angle is 50°. At 30° latitude, angle is 40°.

GLASS

There is little doubt that glass is still the best glazing material. Thermopane is a double-wall glass panel, sealed at the factory so that there is no condensation between the layers of glass. Thermopane is expensive but thinking ahead to the resale value of your property, it may be a good investment.

The next option is to install two layers of glass yourself with weep holes in the frame to help remove the condensation (Figure 10). When the moisture-laden air in the grower drops in temperature, the water vapor condenses on the glazing, which is usually the coldest surface. If there is a lot of condensation when you go into the grower in the morning, turn on a fan, or if you have back-up heat, raise the temperature. With good air circulation you will have less condensation.

There are several types of glass varying in thickness and strength, and for the home solar grower I would suggest tempered glass. It is always surprising to toss a stone at tempered glass and see it bounce off! This suggests that if you have children playing in the solar grower area, tempered glass is a wise investment.

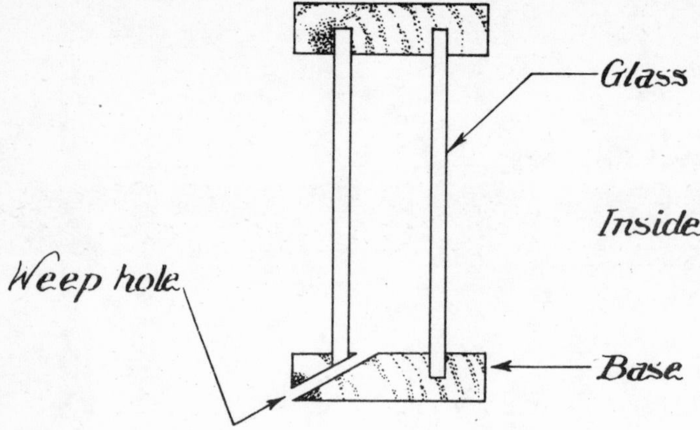

Figure 10. Double-glazing weep holes.

Glass admits about 90 percent of daylight, which is about 10,000 foot-candles. Most people forget that even on a cloudy day there is considerable solar radiation and your solar grower will show a heat gain. For example, today is cloudy with intermittent rain and the outdoor temperature is 50°F (10°C). Inside my solar grower the temperature is 70°F (21°C).

As winter approaches, both the duration and the intensity of sunlight decrease, so careful attention to light conditions is necessary to get good growth. Obviously it is important to keep the glazing surfaces as clean as possible to let in an optimum amount of light.

PLASTIC GLAZING

There are several kinds of manufactured, double-layer plastic coverings made of rigid acrylic and polycarbonate resins (Figure 11). These materials are strong and tough but much lighter than glass. They are so much lighter that you can use framing spaced on 4 foot (1.2 m) centers rather than the 2 foot (.6 m) spacing which is usual for glass. These materials admit about the same amount of light as glass and will last twenty-five or thirty years as does glass.

Polyethylene sheeting is a single-layer, translucent material usually used as a temporary covering because it only lasts for two or three years. Ultraviolet light breaks down polyethylene so that even the better grades, which are treated with ultraviolet inhibitors, have to be

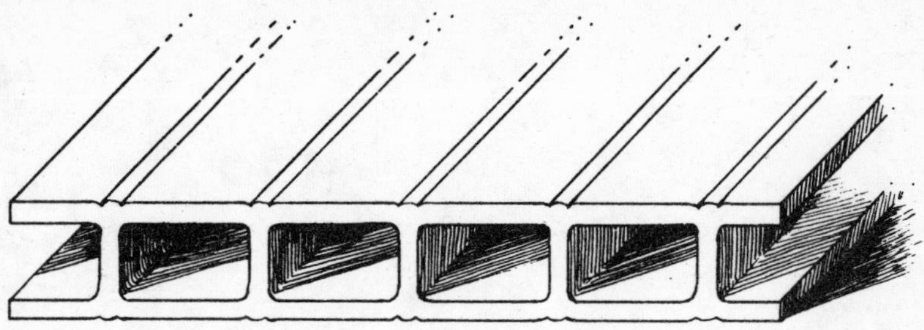

Figure 11. Double-layer acrylic sheeting.

replaced by the third year. The use of double-layer polyethylene is treated in a later chapter.

Fiberglass sheeting is a single-layer, semi-rigid material that is translucent and diffuses the light. Both polyethylene and fiberglass admit about 85 percent of daylight.

If you live in a mild climate where double glazing is not necessary to conserve heat, you might use a fiberglass covering. I have had a fiberglass grower but found I was annoyed by the noise of heavy rain on the roof.

Light Requirements

Using any of the glazing materials mentioned above will give you enough light for good growth. Plants differ in their light requirements as indicated by the variation in their natural habitats. You may well have plants from all over the world in your solar grower. Some come from the jungle understorey where normal daylight is much less than 10,000 foot-candles, and these foliage plants can grow in 100 to 300 foot-candles of light. Flowering plants will do better at 500 foot-candles and twelve hours per day of light. For the food plants, 1,000 foot-candles and twelve hours per day of light is necessary. Once your solar grower is erected, you can watch the light and shadow patterns inside and place plants where the light conditions are most suitable.

If you live where the winter light conditions are poor, you may have to use supplementary fluorescent light in order to get good growth. There are lights available now which closely approximate the spectrum of natural light and are inexpensive to operate.

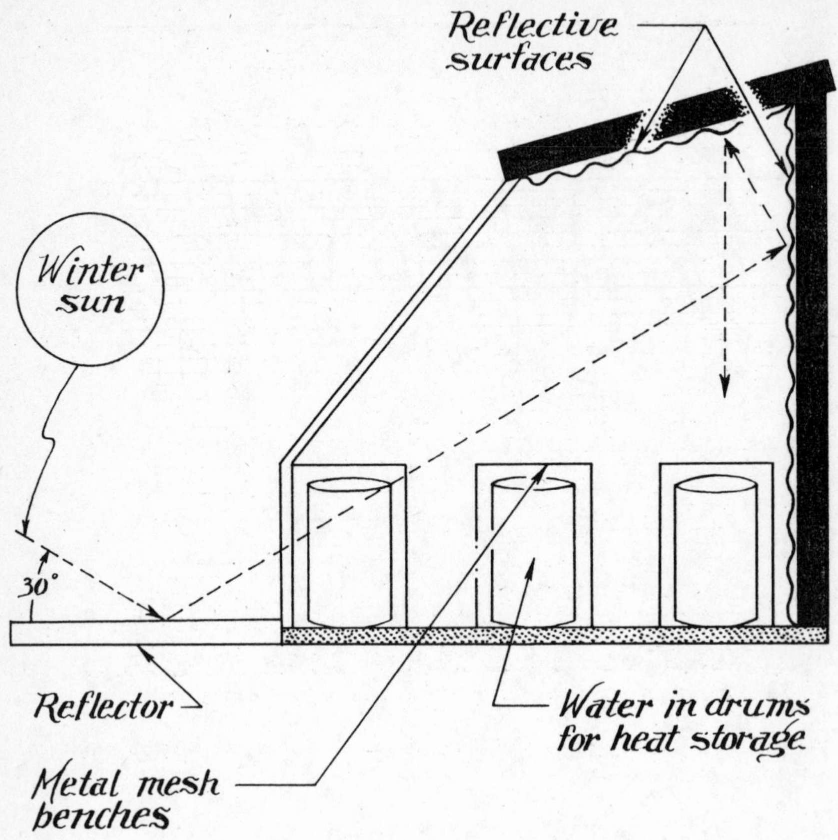

Figure 12. *Reflectors and reflective surfaces add more heat and light to a solar grower, latitude 43° N.*

Reflective Materials for More Light

You can add about one-third more light and heat to the solar grower by using reflective surfaces inside and outside (Figure 12). By putting reflective material on the back wall or under the solid part of the roof, you permit the light to bounce around and strike the heat storage materials. There are several kinds of aluminum-faced paper or foil, and for the roof I use an aluminum-faced insulation board. Almost as good as aluminum foil for this purpose is high gloss white paint, which is probably the best surface for an outside reflector. In snow country you don't need an outside reflector because the snow surface performs the reflective function.

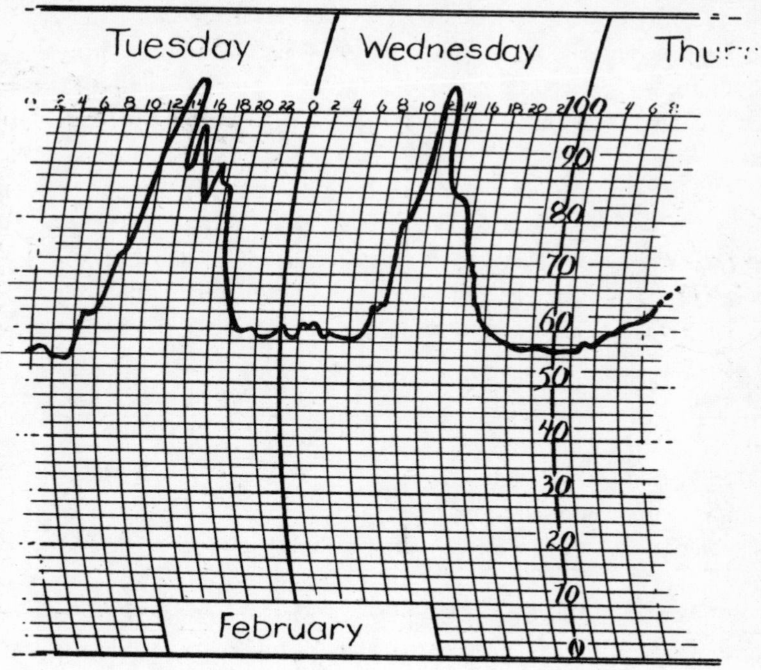

Figure 13. *The heat rise and fall in the author's research solar grower, latitude 43° N.*

Bouncing the light around inside the grower also results in better growth, since light provides the energy for growth.

Before you do anything with reflective materials, or supplementary light, experiment to see what you can grow with natural light only. At 43° N latitude in Canada, I have been able to grow a wide variety of foliage and flowering plants, as well as fruits and berries, using only natural light with no reflective surfaces inside the solar grower.

Heat Storage Materials

Once you get the light and heat into your solar grower, you need the proper storage materials to absorb the heat and hold it for release at night. Materials with enough mass absorb heat during the day so that the solar grower never becomes overheated. The temperature may go up to 100°F (38°C), but it only stays that high for a few minutes. As the heat storage materials absorb the heat, the temperature comes rapidly down to normal (60°F/15.6°C). If you put enough heat storage material in the solar grower you can maintain growing temperatures through the night. I am able to keep my solar grower at an average night temperature of 50°F (10°C) right through a Canadian winter (Figure 13).

Currently, the available heat storage materials are water, rock or masonry and hydrated salts such as sodium sulphate. The relative capacity of these materials to absorb and release heat, when the temperature goes up 10° and then down 10°, is shown in the following table. The heat gain is expressed in Btu (British Thermal Units).

Material	**Btu stored per cubic foot**
Water	625
Rock, 2½ inches (6 cm) diameter	200
Hydrated salts, sodium sulphate	9500
One solar tile, 2 feet by 2 feet (.6m by .6m)	880

With a 30°F (16°C) temperature rise, 1 pound (450 g) of hydrated salt stores 128 Btu. It takes about 4 pounds (1.8 kg) of water or 20 pounds (9 kg) of rock to store 128 Btu.

Let's consider each of these storage materials in greater detail.

WATER

Any kind of container filled with water and painted black will absorb solar heat. If the container is metal, so much the better, as the metal will also absorb heat. In my own solar grower I use 50 gallon (227 l) oil drums, full of water, painted with flat black rust-proof paint. I use the barrels to support the benches which are made of metal mesh sheeting. These open-mesh metal benches allow the light and heat to go directly to the barrel surface and because the bench surface is also metal, it absorbs heat as well (Figure 14). Rectangular containers will stack better than oil drums and allow you to get more storage material in a given space (Figure 15). If you use second-hand containers, make certain that they did not formerly contain toxic chemicals which might volatilize into the air and damage plants. Small containers are really better than big containers because with a large volume of water, there is a tendency for the top to get hot and the bottom to stay cool. Water heat storage absorbs sun heat rapidly enough so that you don't need to ventilate in the winter. Opening and closing the door, daily, supplies enough air exchange.

Figure 14. Open mesh metal bench.

Figure 15. Heat storage in rectangular containers full of water.

You can make or buy fiberglass tubes or tanks for water storage. Such tanks have to be painted black to get the best heat absorption, or you can dye the water black. You can make tubes by rolling sheets of fiberglass and sealing them with resin. What you use for water storage is determined by what is available where you live. If the budget permits, you can have custom-made, galvanized metal containers which fit exactly under the benches.

Almost anywhere you can find black plastic bags to make what I call a solar pillow. As an experiment, fill a small plastic bag one-half full of water and record the temperature of the water. Close the top with two turns of soft wire twisted tight with pliers. Now place the bag behind double glazing in the sun for an hour and then record the temperature again. You will be surprised! I have done this at a room temperature of 65°F (18°C) and had the water reach 100°F (38°C). I use solar pillows in little corners that the sun strikes and between pots or rows of plants on the benches or staging. Your ingenuity may suggest other ways to use water to store sun heat, but remember, the container or the water should be black in order to absorb the optimum amount of heat.

ROCK OR CONCRETE

A common practice is to make the back wall of the solar grower out of concrete blocks painted black, unless the existing wall of the house is masonry. Such a wall will absorb even more heat if the cavities in the blocks are filled with concrete. This increases the amount of mass available for heat storage.

There are several problems with using rock for heat storage in a system such as that outlined under foundations in this chapter.

1. Rock is becoming less and less readily available.

2. From the chart on page 24 you can see that you need twice as much rock, with three times the weight, to store the same amount of Btu as water.

3. The weight and bulk of rock can lead to some tough problems in the construction of the solar grower and may well reduce the area devoted to growing.

For these reasons, I would suggest that you use water or hydrated salts for heat storage.

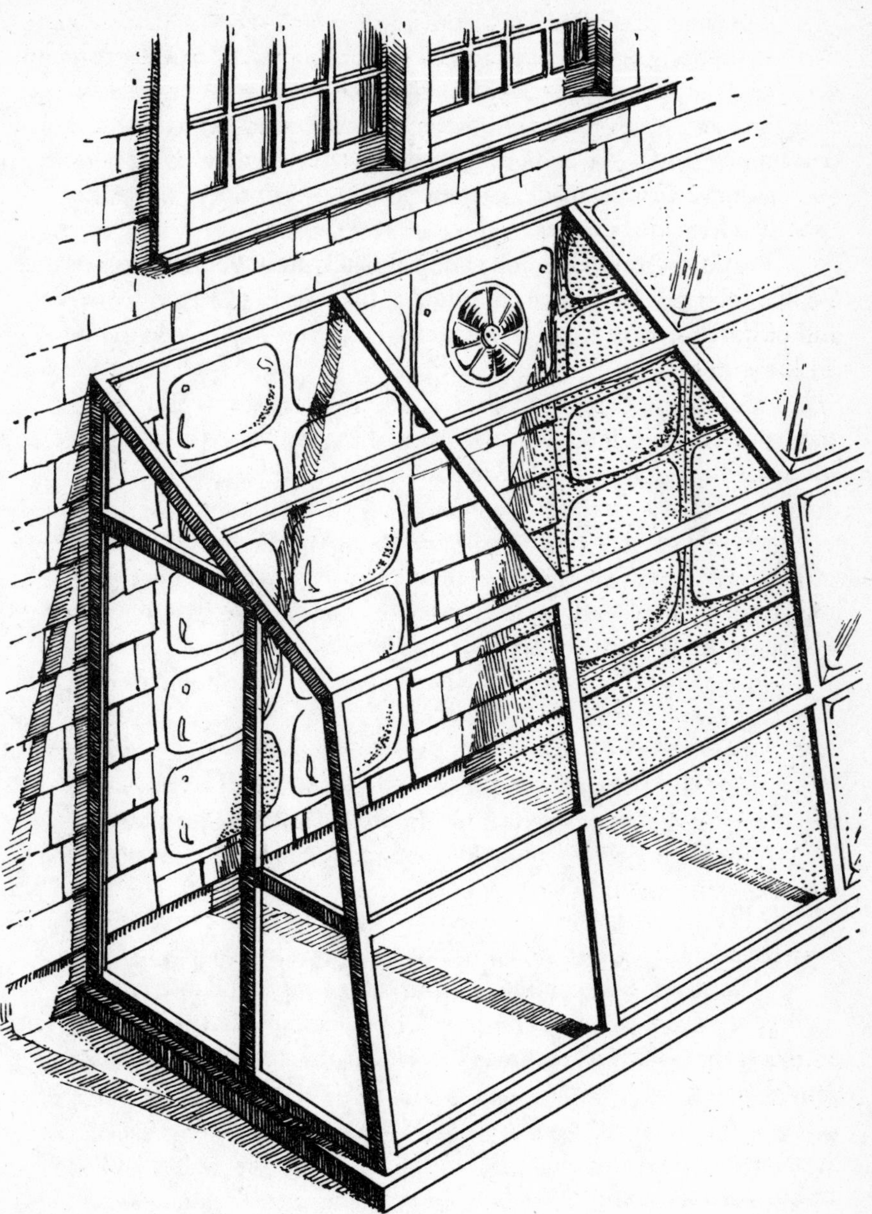

Figure 16. *Hydrated salt heat storage pods.*

HYDRATED SALTS

Millions of tons of hydrated salts occur as natural deposits in Saskatchewan. The chart on page 24 shows that they have the ability to store many times the heat absorbed by water. Hydrated salts are very caustic and must be permanently sealed in heavy, dense plastic containers. When temperatures are down the salt is a solid. As hot air passes over the surface of the container, the temperature goes up until the salt becomes a liquid and begins to store heat. When the salt cools it changes back to a solid, releasing stored heat. This is known as a phase change and is similar to what happens when water becomes ice.

Currently hydrated salt heat storage devices are not readily available. I have talked with several manufacturers of these devices and have found that because demand declined during the eighties, their stocks are now low. One company will remanufacture as soon as there is sufficient demand for the product. Another has been actively looking for the raw materials to produce a hydrated salt heat storage device which may well be on the market now, so keep asking your solar supplier. The hydrated salt units store so much more heat per unit of weight and surface area that they are more suitable than either water or rock.

For storing heat in a water container, one of the best units is Sun-Lite HP, a fiberglass tube specially engineered to resist the causes of molecular deterioration often fatal to some plastics. When filled with clear water the tubes admit light and for decorator purposes you can add black, yellow, bronze or blue in non-toxic dyes.

The hydrated salt heat storage pods shown in Figure 16 can be mounted on the back wall of the attached solar grower to receive the direct rays of the sun. Thermal rods can be mounted in the same way or contained in a heat storage chamber with thermostatic controls, as shown in Figure 17. This is an active solar system involving electricity which can be supplied by readily available photovoltaic panels.

The solar heat tile may not be readily available but will come back on the market as demand warrants. Check with your solar supplier for this and other new heat storage devices which are bound to come along as people discover that they help to reduce heating costs (Figure 18).

There are many other materials which show promise for storing

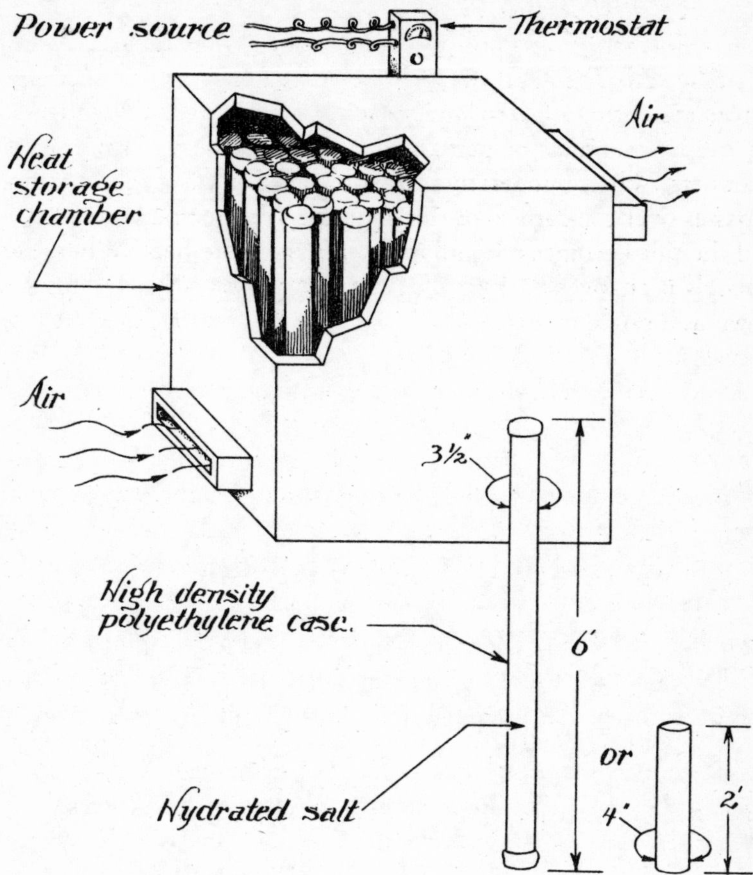

Figure 17. Thermal rods in a heat storage chamber.

heat. One of these is zeolite, a natural clay, commonly used in the petroleum industry. Canadian research indicates that zeolite can store twice as much heat as hydrated salts and does not require insulation to hold the heat for an indefinite period. The Japanese are experimenting with Norbordiene, and Israel is researching calcium chloride hexahydrate. It is just a question of time until the right storage material makes solar energy very attractive for general use. The ultimate objective is to store enough solar heat during the summer to last all through the winter, so that we become independent of all other heat sources.

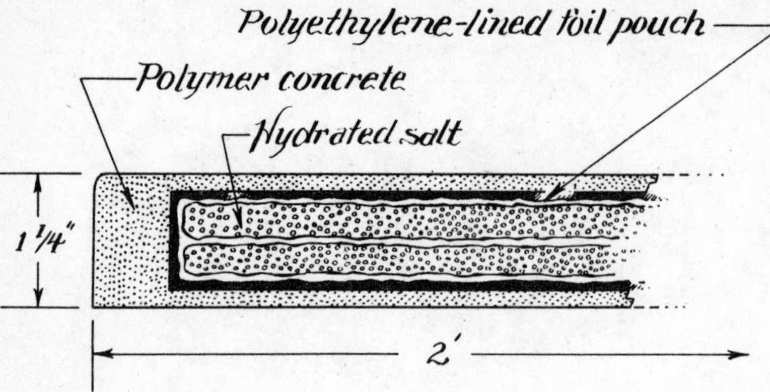

Figure 18. Solar heat tile.

How Much Heat Storage?

How much water storage do you need in your solar grower for winter crops? We can make some general estimates, as indicated in the following table, but there are so many microclimates and local influences on weather that these figures are really only suggested quantities.

City	Insulation, back wall and roof	Water in gals. (litres) per sq. ft. (.09 m^2) of double glazing
Johannesburg Sydney Jacksonville Houston	R-6	2 (9 1)
San Francisco New York Madrid Naples British Isles	R-12	4 (18 1)
Toronto Hamburg	R-24	6 (27 1)
Far North or South	R-40	10 (45 1) or more

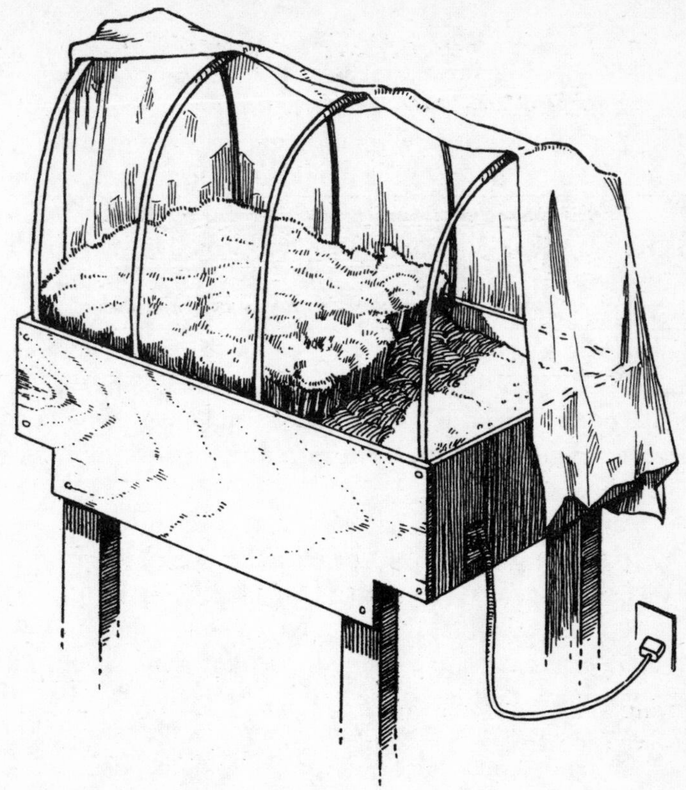

Figure 19. Tented bench to save heat

I have 6 gallons per square foot (27 l per .09m^2) of exposed double glazing in my solar grower, at 43° N latitude, and grow all the winter salad greens using only the heat of solar radiation. I have also tried growing a variety of plants at less than normal temperatures. There is no good data on the low temperature tolerance of many flowers and vegetables, so you have to experiment for yourself. I am certain that more plants than you might think can be grown at 40°F (4°C) night temperatures.

I put 28 hydrated salt heat storage tubes along the back wall of the 10' x 14' (3.05 m x 4.27 m) greenhouse at Longwood Gardens. On a sunny day these tubes absorb about 70,000 Btu during the day, and when the nighttime temperature falls the tubes release heat to keep the greenhouse warm. Even on a cloudy day there is considerable solar radiation.

HEAT RECOVERY

Many people have increased the insulation in their houses to save on heating costs, but relatively few have discovered heat recovery. I used to attend parties with a thermometer in my pocket and ask the hosts if I could take the temperature at the ceiling and then again on the floor. Every time I did this I found the ceiling 10 to 15°F (5-6°C) warmer than the floor. So I would suggest installing a ceiling fan to recover and reuse the heated air. For the home greenhouse I have often installed a decorative tube in the corner with a small squirrel cage fan at the top to blow the warm air down through the tube to the floor, or back onto thermal heat storage units. Recovering heat in both residence and greenhouse saves money on heating costs, especially if you can store the heat in water or hydrated salts.

Another suggestion for using heat efficiently is the heated bench. You don't have to heat the entire grower. You can put a polyethylene tent over a single bench and only use heat for a small area (Figure 19). At most garden shops and nurseries, you can purchase a heat cable commonly used for propagation, with a built-in thermostat set at 70°F (21°C). Installed under the soil in the bench, this will give you an air temperature in the tent of 70°F (21°C). Using this method, I have grown tomatoes and cucumbers in a solar grower where the temperature outside the tented bench went down to 42°F (6°C).

As carefully as you plan, there may well be times when you want extra heat. I use a small fan-driven electric heater, which costs about twenty-six cents per day to keep the solar grower at 52°F (11°C) during sub-zero weather.

Keeping the Heat In

The first consideration is insulation. We have already discussed insulating the foundation. The solid portion of the roof, solid walls and the door can all be insulated with rigid insulation board with the proper R value as indicated in the previous charts. I like to insulate the back half of each gable end using a transparent panel fastened to the inside of the glass frame. This panel is flexible, double-layer polypropylene with an R factor of three. This is not a high R factor, but the material admits 73 percent of daylight and at the same time gives insulation value.

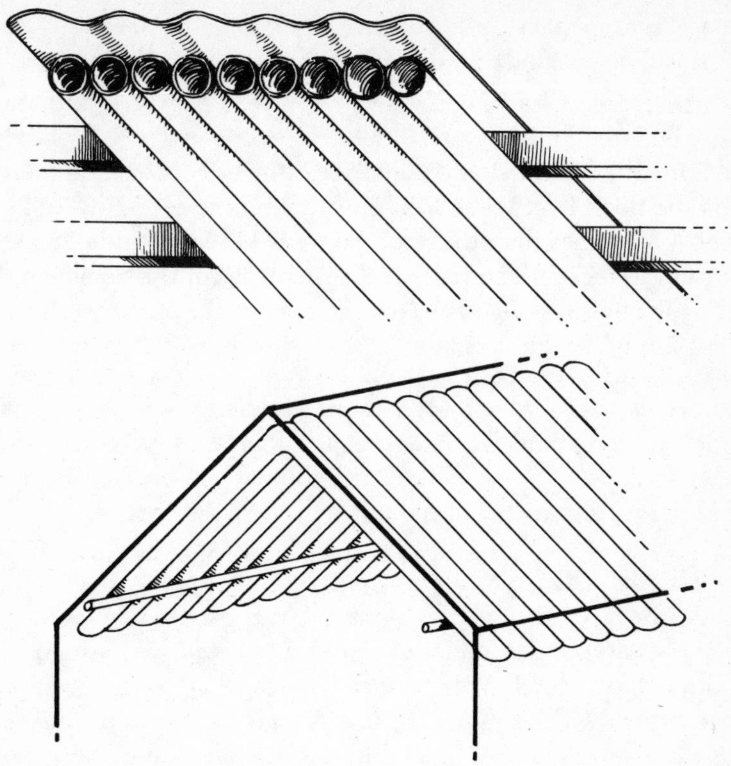

Figure 20. Air blanket insulation.

To eliminate the nighttime heat loss, you need curtains inside which are easy to operate. No one wants to go outside in cold windy weather to install a set of coverings over the glazing. Fortunately, there are at least two types of inside curtains which work very well.

The inflatable air blanket is a sheet of 4 inch (10 cm) polyethylene tubes held under the roof and against both gable ends by wires (Figure 20). It comes in widths up to 6 feet (2 m), which have an overlap flap so that you get a complete seal, and in any length up to 500 feet (150 m). Commercial growers are reporting heat savings of 40 percent by using the air blanket as a winter cover.

When the weather turns cool in the fall, you install the air blanket and leave it up all winter, day and night. You don't have to fuss with curtains or panels every evening! The light goes through the polyethelene tubing, strikes inside surfaces and turns to heat. The heat is effectively trapped and light transmission is reduced by only 10 percent. Some commercial growers find that even with this light reduction they are able to produce good flowering and fruiting crops.

You can inflate the air blanket with a bicycle pump or air mattress pump, using cool air so as to avoid condensation. There is no reason why you can't leave the air blanket up all year round, except that you can't see out through the roof. In summer it will provide insulation against heat. This is one of the better means of controlling heat because it requires so little attention.

Another roll-up curtain, used in a similar manner, is a reinforced sheet with foil on one side and black polythelene on the other. This comes in widths up to 24 feet (7 m) so that a single sheet might cover the entire glazing area. This curtain should be lowered as soon as the sun goes down to prevent heat loss. The foil surface, facing the inside of the solar grower, will reflect the heat already inside.

HEAT MIRROR

In the past ten years there have been considerable improvements in the insulating qualities of greenhouse glazing and windows. Heat Mirror has a metallic-plastic membrane applied to the glazing which admits the solar light energy and reflects heat inward. This film lets the short-wave radiation in and blocks the long-wave heat radiation so that it cannot escape to the outside. This and other innovations are often marketed as low emissivity, or insulated glazing. In terms of thermal resistance, this means you can have R4 or R6 glazing instead of the common R2 material. Using this type of glazing greatly increases the efficiency of the solar greenhouse as a heat trap.

Benches and Staging

In the custom solar grower you can have ground beds, provided the foundation is well insulated to keep the soil warm enough for good root growth. The ground bed is the ideal place for large plants such as fruit trees, grapes and tall plants such as cucumbers. For smaller plants I prefer the raised bed.

It is much easier to have a growing bed at counter level where you can work without bending over. This gives you a bench with soil almost 3 feet (1 m) deep in a concrete box which acts as heat storage material. This type of bench provides high enough soil temperatures to do propagation as well as to grow the root crop vegetables. You should build a trap door near the bottom so that when you want to change the soil every two years, it is easy to shovel out the old soil. There are many advantages to growing in compost made from kitchen table scraps and this type of bench is suitable for a compost-growing medium.

You might wish to install an automated hydroponic bench. Hydroponics is the art of growing plants in a nutrient water solution without soil. This growing technique is becoming increasingly popular and many people get better yields, particularly of tomatoes. I am currently using such a bench and find that by feeding a standard hydroponic formula plus 100 percent emulsified fish fertilizer, I get tomatoes of excellent quality all winter. Automating the bench means that it requires less attention. You can go away for extended periods and come back to find the plants in good condition.

There are corners in the solar grower where staircase staging provides excellent light exposure for growth. If you watch the light and shadow patterns in the grower you can place the shade-loving plants and the sun-lovers in the appropriate locations for good growth. Wood is the best material for this type of staging. A slat surface allows air to circulate and gives you good drainage.

You can use shelves along the edge of a sill, against a wall, or even hanging from a ceiling in the right location. Some plants, such as strawberries and tomatoes, grow very well in hanging baskets which you can position for easy harvesting of the crop. There is also a wide variety of very colorful tropical plants, such as jasmine, columnea and aeschynanthus, which give you the green feeling.

Flooring

See details of different types of floors in the following chapter.

Figure 21. Home-built free-standing solar grower.

Chapter 3

BUILDING A FREE-STANDING SOLAR GROWER

WHEN YOU BUILD your own free-standing structure, the possibilities for size and shape are almost unlimited. You can fit your particular landscape setting with an A-frame, gazebo, roll-top or any design you wish. You can provide space for family living as well as gardening and even have a combination swimming pool and solar garden. Be sure to check local building ordinances before you start, in case you need a building permit.

Size

The first consideration for your solar grower is size. Building your own means you are not restricted to the few sizes manufactured for the prefabricated market. You do not have to deal with a structure that must be taken apart and packed in a box to be shipped over long distances. How do you decide about the size?

First, take inventory of what your family wants to do in the solar garden structure. A good clue is the size of your present house. If you are comfortable in small cozy spaces, then a small grower will do. If you like to spread out, or if you have several children, build a larger grower so that everyone in the family can enjoy growing plants. If you can't decide on a size, build a grower that you can add on to at a later date.

Many folks do not realize that when you double the size of a structure, you are not necessarily doubling the price. If you plan to build an 8 by 12 (2.4 by 3.7m) grower, calculate the cost and do the same for a 16 by 12 (4.9 by 3.7m). You may be surprised to find that the cost does not double. It's wise to do some calculations before you trap yourself in a grower so small that you are constantly frustrated. You may well want to provide room enough for a breakfast nook-type of dining area in the solar grower. Plan to visit greenhouses of different sizes, walk around in them and see how you feel before you decide on a size to build.

Design

Don't be timid about doing your own designing! With graph paper and a ruler you can lay out dimensions and structure to arrive at the particular size and arrangement which best suit your desires. A schematic plan for an ideal solar grower, considering the present state of the art of using sun energy, is shown in Figure 22. The heat storage chamber shows thermal rods but it would accommodate rock or water storage as well. The plan is based on my own experience over a forty-year period, which includes visiting and talking with hundreds of solar innovators in many parts of the world.

The floor plan is an expression of individuality, just as it is for your home, and the schematic design shown in Figure 23 is to help you get started doing your own layout.

Foundation

There is no good substitute for a concrete block or poured wall that goes down below the frostline. If you plan to use heat storage under the floor, then you should pour a slab, and insulate, under the storage area. If you add iron reinforcing to a poured wall, you are increasing the value of the wall for heat storage. And if you can locate the solar grower on a slope facing the equator, then you can take advantage of the insulating value of an earth berm.

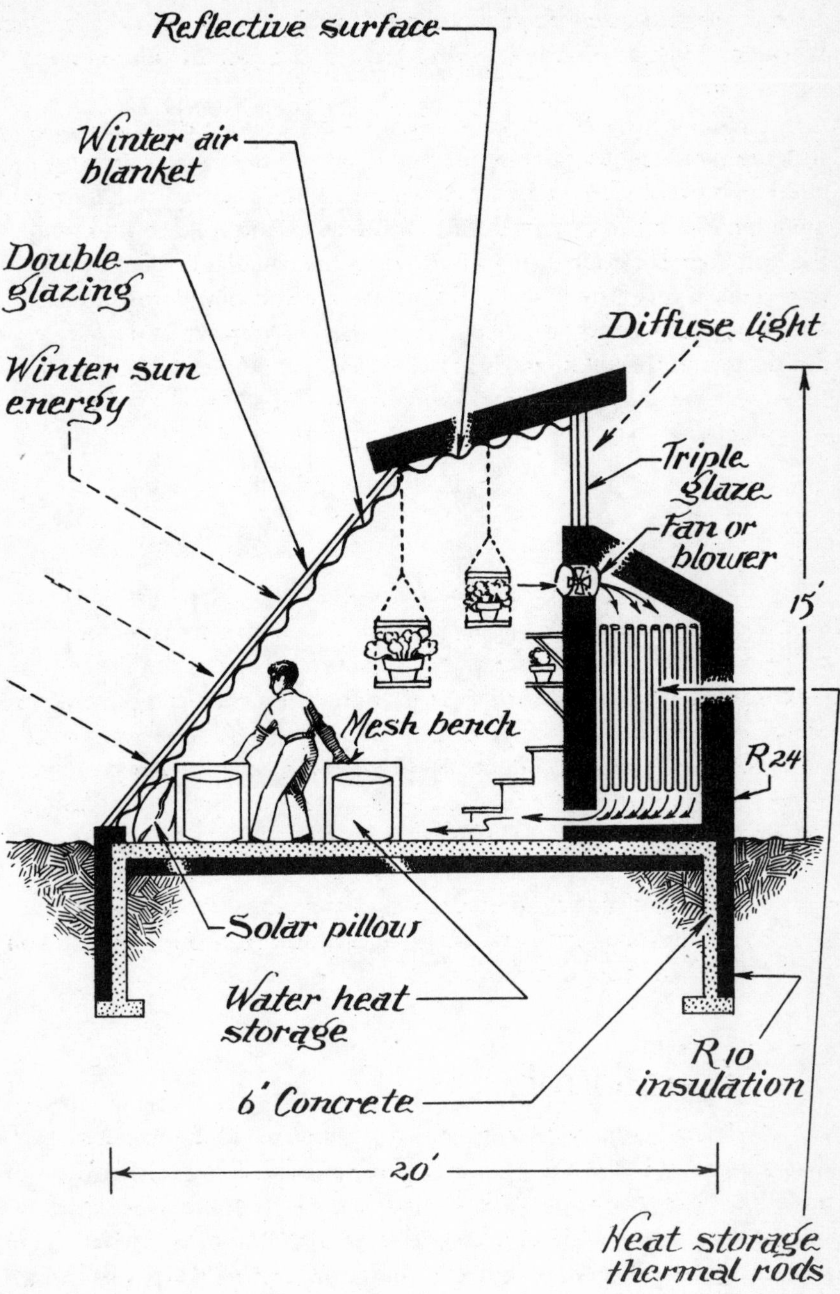

Figure 22. Passive-active solar grower.

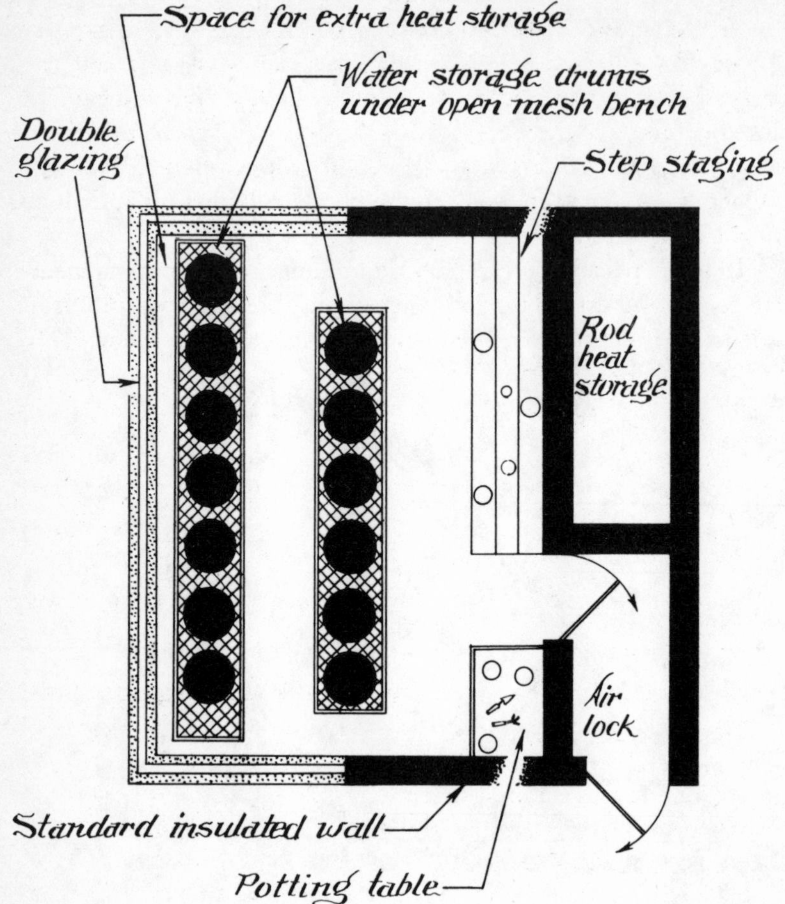

Figure 23. Floor plan for a solar grower.

Frame

Wood is undoubtedly the best framing material. You might use cedar, redwood, cypress, beech, kahika, yellow wood, fern pine or eucalyptus, depending on where you live. A wood frame will last longer if you treat it with a wood preservative, but be careful to avoid products that are toxic to plants. Wood preservatives containing copper naphthenate come in green or a variety of wood tones, and are safe for plants. Zinc naphthenate is also non-toxic to plants, and may be clear as well as tinted. If you have pressure-treated wood available, you can save the time and effort required to treat your own wood. If you want to paint the framing to match the house, use paints with organic oil rather than a lead base. You will find it easier to give the individual structural members a priming coat before you assemble them so that you have no unpainted corners and crevices. I would suggest that you bolt the frame together so that it is easy to extend the solar grower whenever you wish. Once the frame is up, you can use butyl caulking to fill any joints that might hold water.

In many places you can have aluminum or steel framing members cut to size and drilled for you to assemble. The only real problem with the metal frame solar grower is the heat loss through the metal itself. It sems like a small thing, but when you add up losses from all the framing members you are losing a lot of heat. For example, the losses by conduction are as follows:

Conductivity	(Btu in hours per square foot (.09 m^2))
Aluminum	1,425
Steel	310
Wood	0.8

To eliminate this heat loss you can apply a foam insulating tape to the inside of the metal framing members. I have found it much easier to work with wood than with metal but where you need a lightweight structure, aluminum is the best solution. There is no reason why you could not use wood for the back of the solar grower and aluminum for the double-glazed surface only.

Glazing

You can glaze with glass, fiberglass, double-wall acrylic sheeting or polyethylene. The considerations mentioned under glazing for the attached solar grower should help you decide which type to use. If you use standard construction that is insulated for the back wall and part of the roof, you will not need as much glazing as in the older types of free-standing greenhouses, so perhaps your budget will permit buying thermopane glass. On the other hand, you can grow vegetables, fruit and flowers under fiberglass or polyethylene just as well as you can under glass. So if you don't mind not being able to see out, these latter materials are usually less expensive initially than thermopane. But if you calculate the cost per year that the material lasts, glass is still probably the cheapest glazing.

Insulation

Between the studs and rafters you can use fiberglass blanket or any other insulation that will not absorb moisture. Cover this with foil-faced rigid insulation board to provide a vapor barrier as well as a reflective surface. The total R value should add up to twenty. For very cold areas I would add a second sheet of rigid insulation.

For winter growing, use the inflated air blanket to prevent heat loss through the glazing. The air lock entry (Figure 23) will keep cold air from rushing into the grower and will also provide a place to store tools and materials for gardening.

Heat Storage

In order to retain as much growing and living space as possible, you should consider using hydrated salts (if they are available) for heat storage. You do not want a solar grower that is messy and cluttered, which is often the feeling you get when you walk into a grower full of all sizes and shapes of water containers. Installing water containers under the benches is a good solution in a solar grower. If the solar greenhouse is primarily for recreation and relaxation, then water tubes set against a wall will give you room for chairs and other furniture.

To get maximum heat absorption, you should install a small fan in the peak of the grower, which will circulate the air back down over the heat storage material. This can be a low velocity fan, no more than a foot (.3 m) in diameter, which revolves very slowly to move air rather than blow it with great force.

Special Structures

Whatever the reason, you may want a solar grower that is entirely unique. For many people, it is as much fun to come up with architectural innovations as it is to experiment with solar methods. Let's take a look at what some people are doing.

A-FRAME

An A-frame is easy to build, requires relatively little material and will shed snow very well. There is a lot of space in the top where

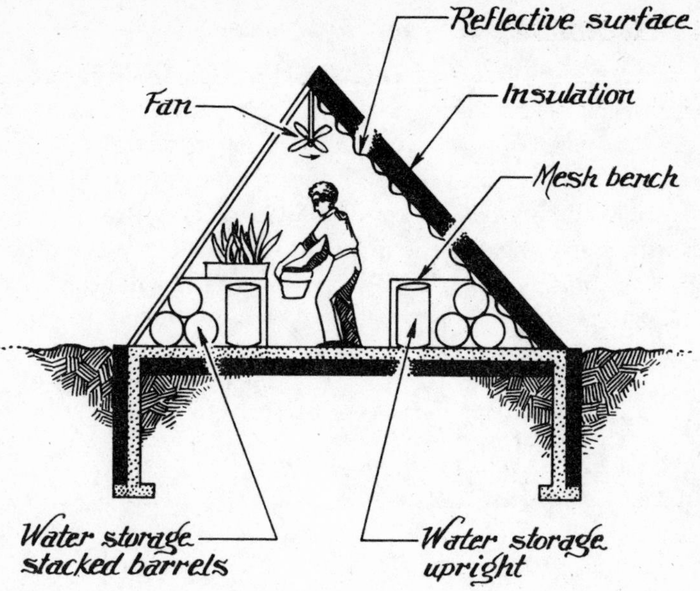

Figure 24. A-frame solar grower.

you can place hanging baskets or shelves. This is the warmest part of the A-frame and would be a good area for tropical plants (Figure 24). On the negative side, you are cramped for room, especially if you are 6 feet (183 cm) or taller.

THE ROLL-TOP

This is an ingenious homemade design using plywood as the sheathing (Figure 25). The side facing the equator has clear double-glazed, hard-surfaced plexiglass set in curved, laminated arches. At night, the roll-top cover comes down to keep the night heat in. This cover is made of insulated, corrugated fiberglass which fits the curve nicely. The back of the roll-top has shelves on the outside for pots and gardening necessities.

The heat storage chamber might have rock, water or hydrated salt rods with a small blower to assist natural convection and take air through the heat storage material.

This type of solar grower would blend very well with modern residential architecture. An attractive structure will add to the resale value of your property.

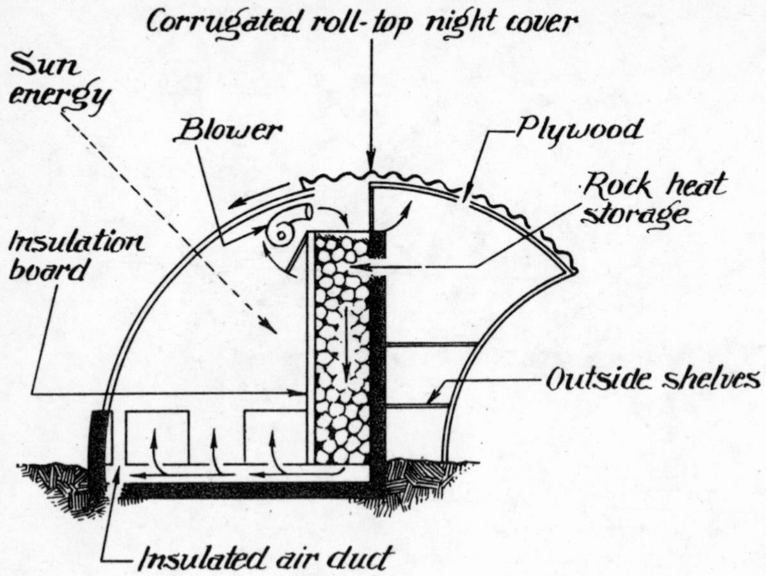

Figure 25. Roll-top solar grower.

THE SOLAR SHED

You probably have a storage shed in the backyard at present. For a very modest sum, you can convert the shed into a dual purpose structure. You can let in some light for solar gardening and still use the shed for storage (Figure 26).

Many of these storage sheds are made of sheet metal panels bolted together, and have sliding doors. If you remove two or three roof and wall panels, on the side facing the equator, you can replace them with glazing and have a solar grower.

The best glazing material for this purpose is double-wall acrylic or polycarbonate sheeting. This glazing is tough enough so that it won't break when you bump it with tools or equipment. Put the glazing in a wood frame using glazing putty and bolt the frame directly to the metal. To make sure of a weatherproof seal, use butyl caulking between the wood and the metal. If you paint the shed a dark shade of green, it will absorb almost as much heat as a black surface.

If your existing shed is made of wood, then cut out sections of roof and wall as though you were putting in windows or skylights. Put the glazing in a wood frame and install it as you would a window. It is

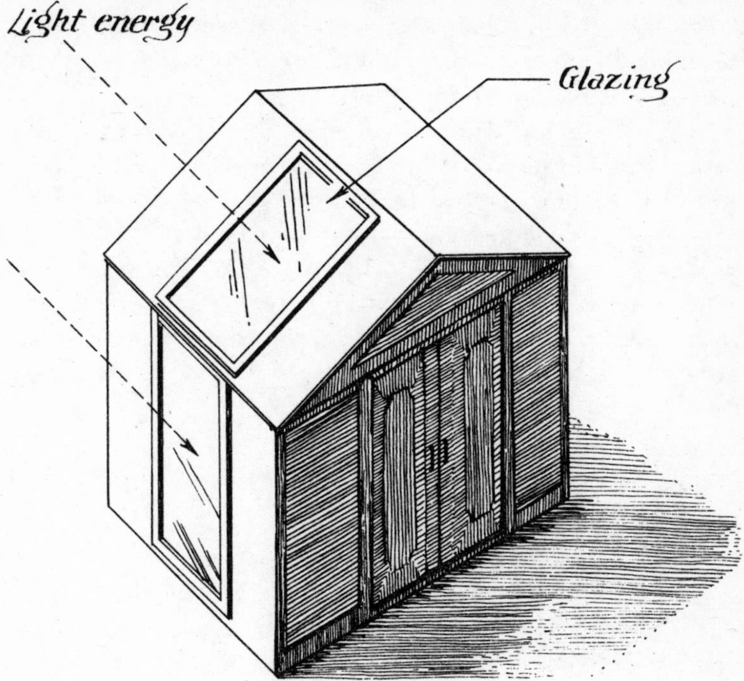

Figure 26. Solar shed.

particularly important to use butyl caulking on the roof glazing to avoid leaks.

This is not the ideal solar grower, but it is a good way to start solar gardening with very little expense. Of course, if you put an appropriate type of heat storage material inside, you can do some winter solar gardening.

Interior Construction

The common materials for the floor of a solar grower are gravel, brick, stepping stones, poured concrete or porous concrete. Solar heat tiles can be used under benches. Gravel is difficult to walk on or travel over with a wheelbarrow full of soil. Brick and concrete stepping stones work very well as long as you keep the surface free of algae by applying a household bleach containing sodium hypochlorite.

If you plan to pour concrete, I would suggest a porous concrete mix which gives a good walking surface and provides excellent drainage. You also get a heat bonus for the solar grower, because porous concrete allows the warm air stored in the ground to rise during the night.

To mix one yard (.75 m^3) of porous concrete, use 2,800 pounds (1270 kg) of ⅜ inch (9.5 mm) crushed rock or pea gravel, six bags of cement, 15 to 18 gallons (68 l to 82 l) of water and no sand. Put in the 15 gallons (68 l) of water. See if the pieces of gravel are well coated with cement; if not, add more water but not more than 18 gallons (82 l). In order to coat the gravel thoroughly, you need a small cement mixer. Add the water cautiously so that you get enough to bind the rock fragments, but no extra soup! After you pour the mix into the forms to make a floor, tamp it down with a board. Do not trowel the surface or you'll lose the porous quality .

Benches and Staging

If you want ground beds for tall plants, try raised beds which keep the soil off the porous concrete walks. The other kinds of staging, benches, tables, shelves, tubs and hanging baskets are just like the furniture in your house. You arrange these features to suit your needs and your decorating taste. Some of the possibilities are shown in Figure 27.

Automation

I like to be able to go away and leave the solar grower for a couple of weeks and come back to find healthy plants. You can do this with automated systems to control heating, watering, feeding and ventilating. Some of these systems are now powered by electricity from solar cells. In the Bibliography, you will find books to help you automate your solar grower.

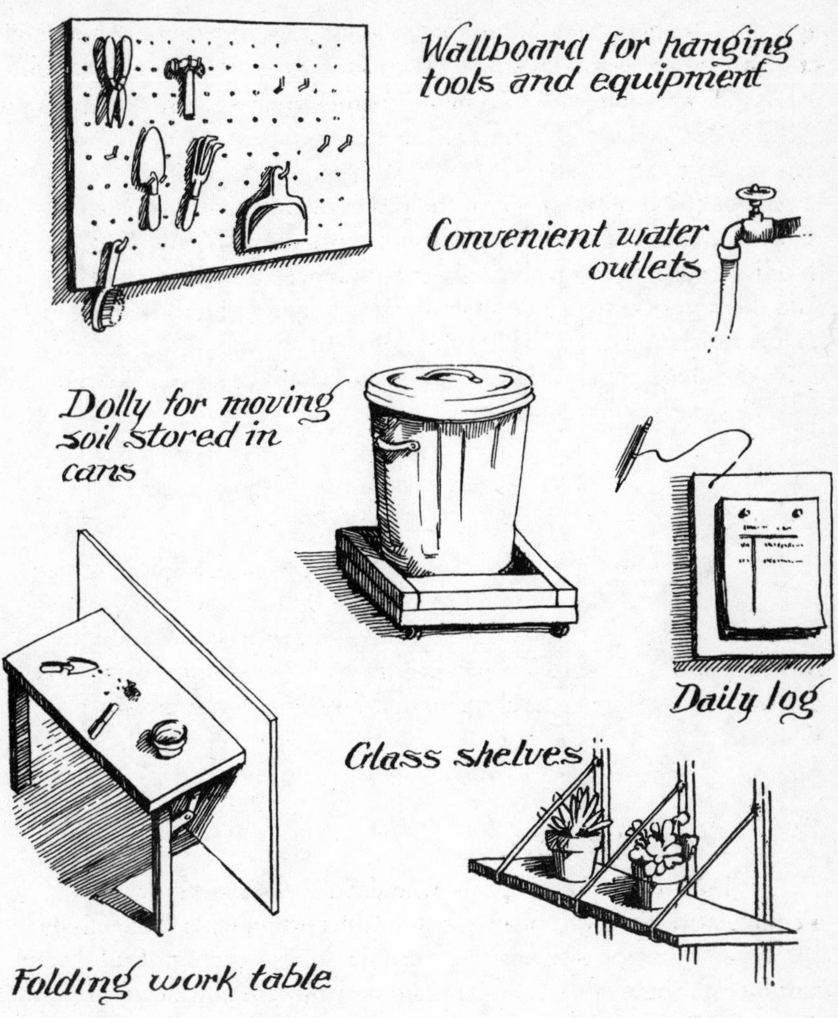

Figure 27. Interior furnishings.

Figure 28. *Reach-in solar grower.*

Chapter 4

PREFABRICATED SOLAR GROWERS

THE FIRST decision you have to make is what type of prefabricated unit you want to convert into a solar grower. Some of the types available are shown in Figure 29. Most prefabricated "greenhouses" are not designed for solar growing.

There are a few companies offering double-glazed structures with hydrated salt heat storage, which they market as a solar greenhouse. With the addition of insulation of the proper type, in the right places, you can convert these structures to acceptable solar growers. Here are some of the problems to watch for:

1. The glazing angle of the structures is not your latitude plus ten degrees, which you need for optimum light conditions.

2. Quite often they come with only single glazing and no easy way of converting to double glazing.

3. Many have no provisions for heat storage materials.

4. Most come without any materials for night covering to keep the heat in.

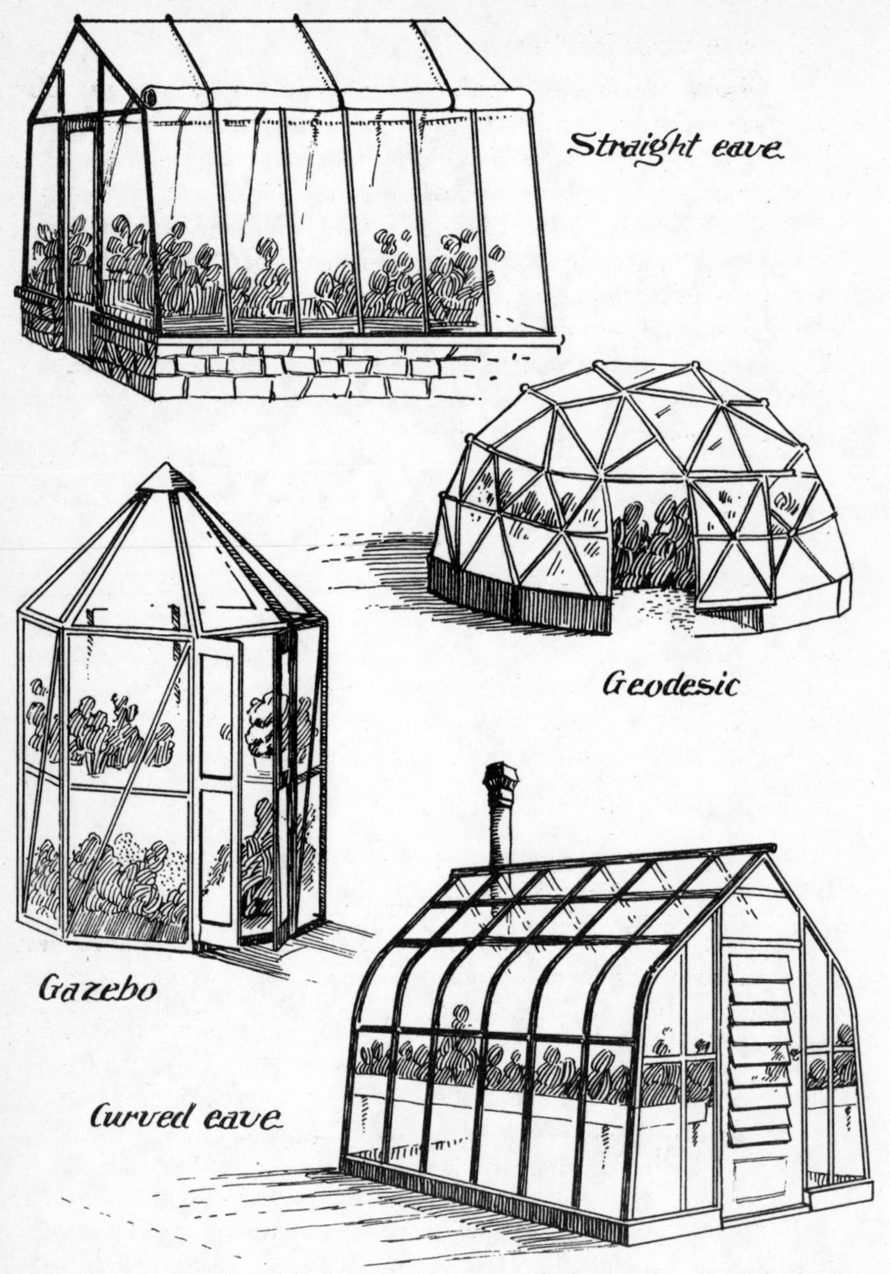

Figure 29. *Special prefabricated structures to adapt for solar growing.*

Orientation

Before you decide what to buy, you should study your particular site to see where you can best locate the structure. Examine the side of the house facing the equator and determine whether a lean-to or an even-span grower will fit best against the house (Figure 30). A lean-to will have the long axis attached to the house, while the gable end, or even-span, will have the short axis against the house. For solar heating, you want as much glazing exposed to the sun as possible. If you cannot locate on the side facing the equator, then the next best orientation is the east side. If there is no appropriate location available, then you should consider a free-standing unit that you can position with the long axis facing the equator.

Foundation

Any of the standard foundations already discussed will do for the prefabricated unit. In mild climates, you can put your frame on top of the ground with no foundation and use anchor legs buried in the soil to hold the structure down. Even then I would suggest that you dig a trench two feet (.6 m) deep along the perimeter of the structure and insulate, so that the ground acts as heat storage material.

Construction

There is at least one prefabricated unit in which the metal components are made with a thermal break so that you do not lose heat to the outside by conduction through the metal. If you can't find this type of frame, then use an insulating tape or sealant, inside, on all the metal framing members.

Adapting for Solar Growing

You are back to the basics of the solar grower. Get the heat in, absorb the heat and keep it inside! If your prefabricated greenhouse has single glass as the glazing material, then you should double glaze to save heat. I have done this by bolting a wood frame to the metal and adding a covering of flat fiberglass. I would suggest 5 ounce (140 g) material with a Tedlar coating. Tedlar is a tough, abrasion-resistant film, which is bonded to the fiberglass so that it maintains its good light transmission characteristic for a longer time than untreated fiberglass. Without this outer film, fiberglass will deteriorate and turn yellow in a few years. In buying fiberglass, make certain that you get a greenhouse grade which admits almost as much light as glass. Construction grades of fiberglass do not admit enough light for good plant growth.

If you have a wood frame prefabricated unit, you can stretch polyethylene over the structure for double glazing during the winter. The polyethylene should be stapled in position. For added strength, nailing strips are then nailed over the staples. There is no satisfactory way to double glaze corrugated fiberglass over a metal frame.

You can apply Aircap or Bubblepak polyethylene on the inside for winter double glazing (Figure 31). This comes in rolls and you can cut pieces to fit between the framing members, directly against the glass. The best fastening is double-faced tape. This type of polyethylene sheeting gives you little bubbles of air, a good type of insulation that will reduce heat loss about 25 percent. In the summer, you take off the Aircap and roll it up for use the next winter.

Another alternative is to install panels of double-wall polypropylene sheeting to the inside of the frame with double-faced tape. These panels will give you better insulation but are more difficult to store through the summer.

Heat Storage

The best alternative to hydrated salt heat storage is probably water in Sun-lite HP fiberglass tubes. There are tubes 1 foot (.305 m) in diameter and 8 feet (2.44 m) tall for mounting along a north wall. The smallest tubes are 1 foot (.305 m) in diameter and 4 feet (1.22 m) tall—these are perhaps the most useful in the home solar grower.

If you place water tubes under the benches I would suggest using expanded metal bench surfaces to admit as much solar radiation directly to the water tubes and as much air movement to the plants as possible (Figure 14).

I would suggest using a non-toxic black dye to color the water in the tubes. The black water container will absorb 35 percent more solar radiation than a clear water tube. Any water container for heat

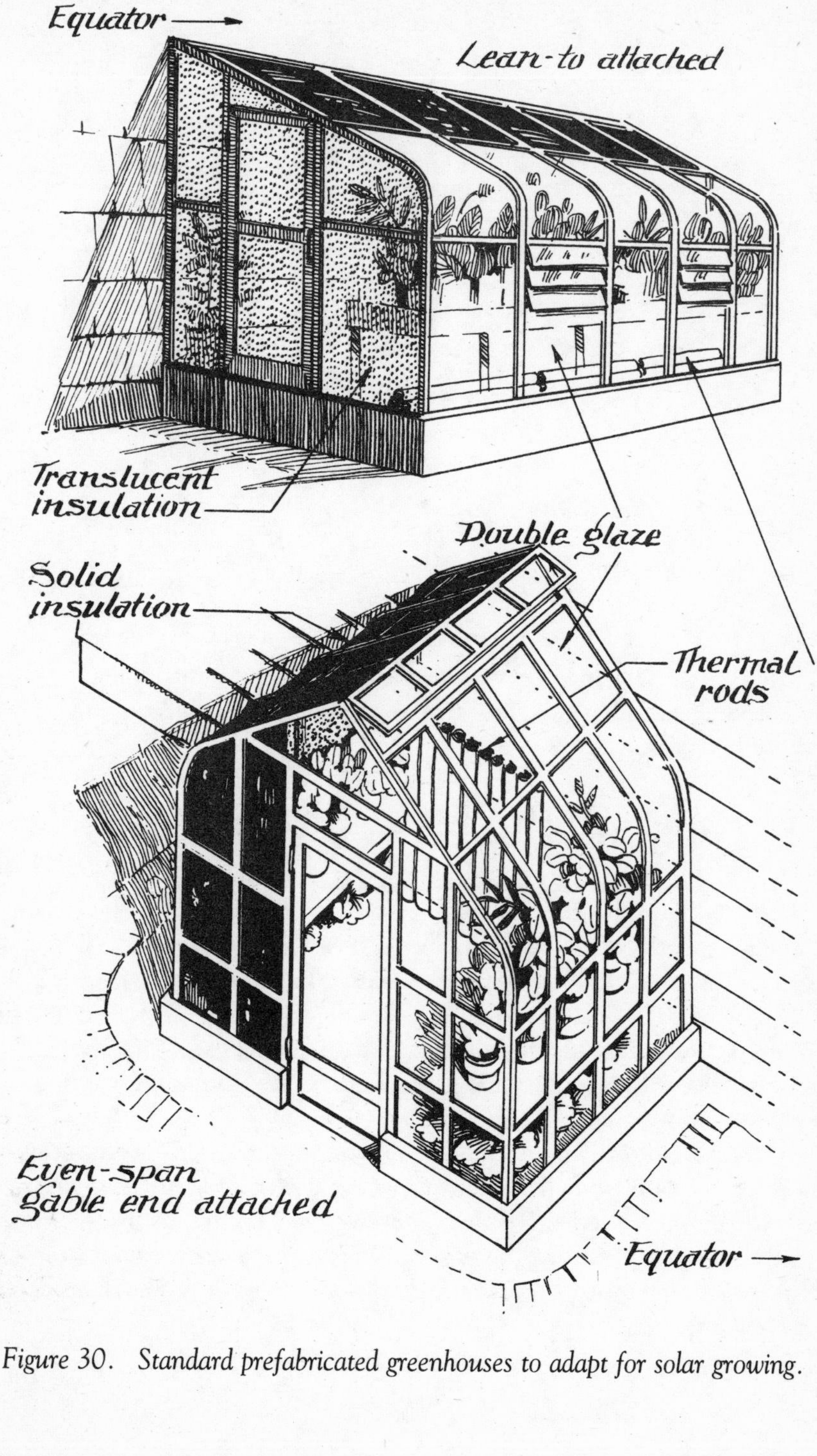

Figure 30. Standard prefabricated greenhouses to adapt for solar growing.

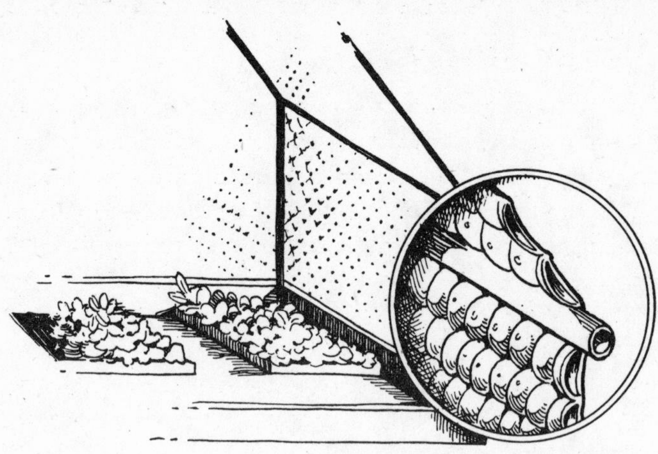

Figure 31. Bubblepak insulation.

storage should be painted black in order to absorb the maximum amount of solar radiation. Ask your solar dealer which black paint is best for heat absorption.

Keeping the Heat In

The back wall and the back roof, away from the equator, should be insulated with material to provide an R factor of twenty. The easiest material to work with is rigid insulation board. If the insulation board is white, rather than foil-faced, you will gain almost as much reflected light as with the foil surface.

You can glue the rigid sheets directly to the glass with the proper wallboard cement. Some glues dissolve the insulation board, so make sure you get the right product.

I have already mentioned using curtains and translucent air blankets to retain heat. If you have a free-standing prefabricated structure, you can use a reflective curtain drawn over the plants from eave to eave for night control of heat loss. This system is widely used in commercial greenhouses to keep the warm air down near bench level during the night.

Advantages of the Lean-To Prefabricated Unit

It takes a lot of courage to put on overshoes and a warm coat to go out in a winter storm to see how the orchids are doing in a free-standing solar grower. It is so much more enjoyable to have direct access to the attached, prefabricated solar grower, so that you can go out in your slippers and shirt-sleeves to enjoy the pleasures of solar gardening.

If your attached unit is properly engineered, you may well have extra heat you can move into your house to help cut down the heating bill. I have a window in my dining room which opens directly into my solar grower. I keep a thermometer on the window sill. Yesterday, the temperature outdoors was 38°F (3°C) and the temperature in the solar grower was 110°F (43°C) under bright sunshine. I opened the window and in a few minutes I had 95°F (35°C) air streaming into the dining room. There was enough heat coming in from the solar grower to keep the dining room at 70°F (21°C) all day, with no other source of heat. Don't overlook the heating value that the attached solar grower can have for the residence.

Other Prefabricated Structures

THE GEODESIC DOME

One of the unique structures for home solar gardening is the geodesic dome. This is a very light, but strong structure which can be glazed with double-wall acrylic sheeting. In many places, you can buy the frame as a kit and do your own glazing. The angle of the glazing is excellent for optimum light and heat penetration. You can cover a large area for less money with a geodesic dome than with any other type of structure. Although there are problems trying to arrange benches in a circular area, you can use pipe framing bent to fit the walls. Solar tiles or thermal rods would be the best way to store heat.

THE REACH-IN SOLAR GROWER

On the small city lot, you may not have room for a walk-in solar grower. If you have 2 to 3 feet (.6 m to 1 m) between a walk and the house, for instance, that is room enough for a prefabricated walk-in unit (Figure 28).

The frame is usually metal, but you could make your own out of 2 by 2 lumber bolted together with galvanized bolts. However, considering the complications of constructing two sliding doors, it is probably better to buy a kit.

To make this a solar grower, I would use solar heat tiles or pods on the back wall. You should use a thermal piston vent, either into the house or outside, because these small structures heat up very rapidly and can burn your plants. Set the thermal piston at 100°F (38°C) and you will store heat without damaging plants. You will get better light distribution if the shelves are open mesh metal or wire mesh. An open pan of water on the floor will help keep the humidity up for good growth.

THE WINDOW SOLAR GROWER

The window solar grower is really an extension of an existing room, which is on such a small scale that there is no room for solar heat storage. Most prefabricated window growers have a frame of aluminum, which makes a light device to attach to the house. If you don't have room for a larger structure to function as a true solar grower, then you can at least grow a few more plants in a window on the sunny side of the house.

Heat builds up rapidly in these small window greenhouses and, again, the best solution is to use a thermal piston vent.

Cautions

Before you buy a prefabricated unit to convert to a solar grower, find out if there is a hobby greenhouse association near you, and visit people who are solar gardening in different kinds of structures.

When your prefabricated unit is delivered, open the cases and check to see that all the parts are there. If something is missing, call the supplier immediately. You can get very frustrated if you discover something missing in the middle of construction!

There are difficulties to converting a prefabricated unit to a solar grower. These problems are not insurmountable but basically, it is better to build your own. If you don't feel up to designing and building your own, employ a competent solar engineer and contractor to do the job for you. You have nothing to lose by getting quotations from two solar companies to see what it costs.

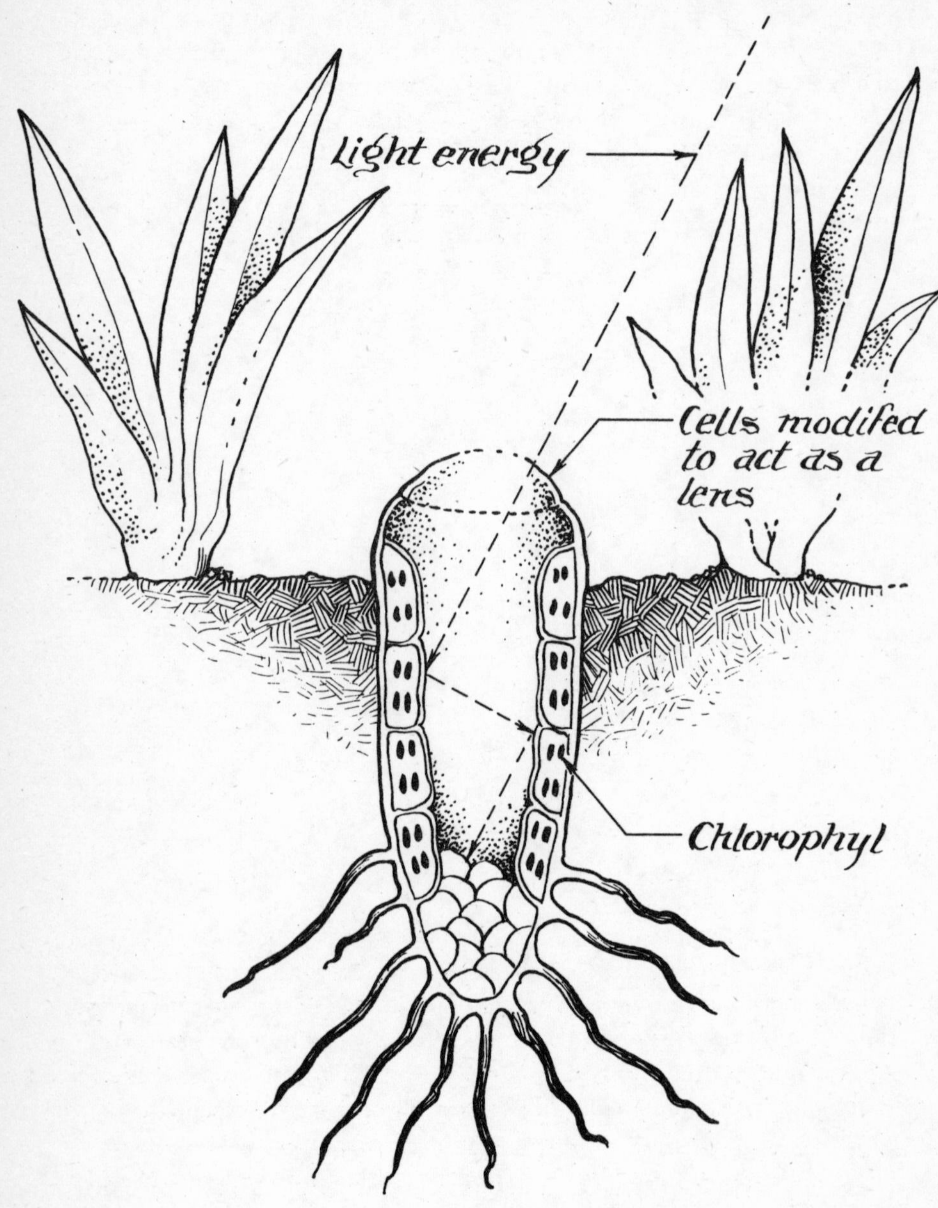

Figure 32. *The* Fenestraria, *or window plant, is a living solar grower.*

Chapter 5

THE SUN PIT

THE ORIGINAL underground solar grower is a living plant from the deserts of South Africa called *Fenestraria*, the window plant (Figure 32). The light shines through lens-like cells in the top of the plant, bounces around inside until it strikes the chlorophyl cells and then releases energy. This is the principle of the solar sun pit (Figure 33).

In many parts of the world you will find people using root cellars to store vegetables for winter. A solar sun pit is much like a root cellar except that the roof admits light. The idea of the sun pit is to get down out of the wind, take advantage of the warmth of the earth and still be able to grow plants. On a tour of the cold latitudes in North America, I found many variations of the sun pit in use, especially for propagation of new plants. Some sun pits had the eave of the roof at ground level; some were partly sunken or, more often, had earth berms piled up to eave level on all sides. The earliest sun pits were hand dug and consisted of a trench with a roof. With the advent of the bulldozer it is not difficult to construct berms around a free-standing grower.

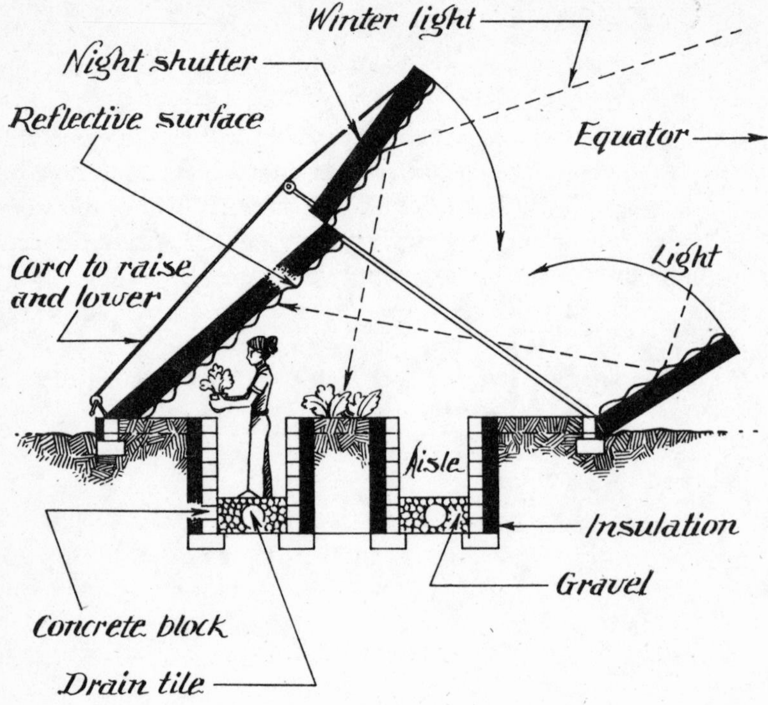

Figure 33. Sun pit.

Location

If you have good loam soil, or any soil that is easy to dig, and if it is well drained so that you won't be standing in water when you are working in the grower, then a sun pit is practicable. The long axis of the sun pit should face the equator, because one of the problems is to get enough light into the structure. The angle of the winter sun is low, so you need proper orientation. If the exposure is correct, you can build the sun pit attached to your house or an outbuilding.

Size

A small sun pit is sheer frustration! After trying such a small pit, I built the second one 16 feet by 20 feet (5 m by 6 m), with the roof ridge 7 feet (2.1m) above the ground. This gives you room for an adequate growing surface, as well as some space for heat storage material.

Construction

You will find plans for sun pits which require excavation of the entire size of the structure to a depth of at least 4 feet (1.2 m), a lot of digging! If you plan this type of structure, it will cost less to build it above ground and have an earth mover push a berm up to eave level. In this way you can adjust the berm to get as much light as you wish. I have found excavating two aisles, and leaving the earth in the center, a lot simpler than digging out the entire structure.

FOUNDATION

Once you have laid out a perimeter of 16 feet by 20 feet (5 m by 6 m), dig a shallow trench for wood forms and a footing for the frame. The rest of the job will be much easier if you take time to level the footing with a piece of lumber and a level.

Excavate each of the aisles 6 feet (180 cm) wide and 5 feet (150 cm) deep so that you have room to lay the concrete block wall. I usually fill the block with concrete mortar and insert reinforcing rods to give the wall extra strength.

To ensure good drainage, put a foot (30 cm) of gravel at the bottom of the aisles with a drain tile to carry the water off.

I found that it was worthwhile to insulate the outer and inner walls of the aisles to hold the sun heat in the grower.

FRAMING

You can use 2 by 4 or 2 by 6 treated wood for the frame. The rafters should be spaced to accommodate the glazing. The important consideration here is the angle of the glazing facing the equator. The back side of the pit grower can be any convenient angle as long as it is insulated to conserve heat.

GLAZING

From the materials available in your area, select the best double glazing. I would suggest polycarbonate sheeting. However, almost anywhere you can find polyethylene sheeting to use for double glazing, which you first staple then nail down with wood strips.

INSULATION

There are so many people, in so many places, doing research on energy conservation that new products appear on the market almost every week. This is true of insulation materials. One of these, for instance, is a granular ceramic material that has an R 70 rating for only a few inches of thickness. It is equivalent to 28 inches (71 cm) of fiberglass or 26 inches (66 cm) of cellulose. Once the granular product is poured, it adheres to itself and to adjacent surfaces, making a unified structural surface which reflects heat. This suggests that you should explore in your vicinity for the availability of the newer insulation developments. At present, ceramic insulation is applied only by franchised contractors, so rigid polyurethane board is the best solution for insulating the roof and foundation if you want to do the job yourself.

On the inside of the back roof, use reflective material to get all the light possible into the solar sun pit.

For night covering you should use reflective shutters on the outside of the sun pit. When open during the day, they will help get more light into the structure. The other alternative is to use the clear polyethylene air blanket, described earlier, particularly if you are in heavy snow country where it is difficult to handle outside shutters.

HEAT STORAGE MATERIALS

There is so little room in a sun pit, with the benches at ground level, that you are dependent on the earth volume under the benches for heat storage. In addition, try putting a bank of solar pillows along the back of the benches below the reflective surface, or hydrated salt containers on the back wall. While earth is not the best heat storage material, you have such a large volume of soil under the benches that you will be able to maintain growing temperatures during the winter.

ENTRYWAY

You should pour a concrete ramp at the door of the sun pit rather than build steps. Steps are difficult to build and a nuisance to navigate with a wheelbarrow full of compost. The ramp should have an air lock covering over it, for the winter. Cold air runs downhill, just like water, and without a cover you'll have a pool of cold air right in front of the door. Every time you open the door you'll dump that cold air into the sun pit.

If you are building an attached solar sun pit, try to arrange for an entrance into the basement of the house. The convenience advantage is substantial. You can use the house foundation wall as one wall of the sun pit and save considerable work and expense (Figure 34).

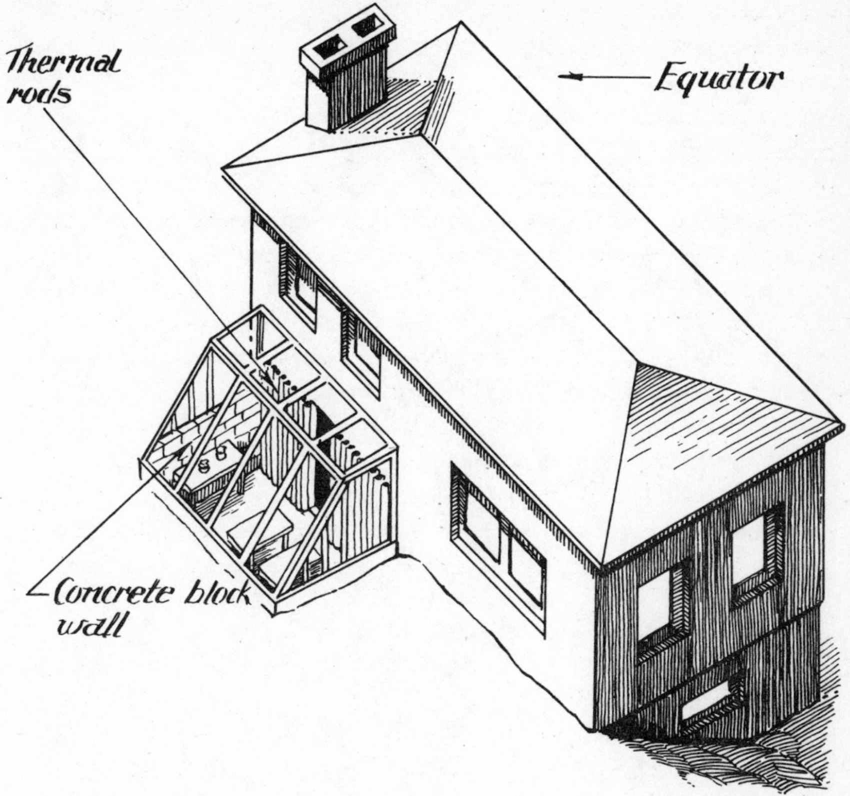

Figure 34. Attached sun pit, using thermal rods against back wall.

DRAINAGE

If you are not certain about the sub-surface drainage, then you should consider putting in drain tile. For even better control of excess water, put a sump about 3 feet deep (1 m) under one of the benches and install a pump to carry off the water.

Figure 35. Solar growing in the bathroom.

Chapter 6

SOLAR GARDEN ROOMS

CURRENT MAGAZINES are featuring articles about letting more light into the residence, primarily to reduce heating costs. Uniformly, these publications overlook the fact that if you let light and heat into a house you can create solar gardens by using reflective surfaces and storing heat in solar tiles, solar rods and pods, or other common materials such as brick, tile, slate or water in containers. Let's look at some of the ways you can do this.

Solar Attic

Normally you might not think of the attic as a room to do anything in, except store paraphernalia. But with skylights, sky domes, roof windows, skyscopes or dormer windows, and heat storage material, you have the things you need for a solar growing room.

Usually, whatever you have stored in the attic can be condensed into a smaller space so that you have room for your new solar attic garden. Many people have transformed the basement into a recreation area for the family. Now, with the new awareness of solar potential, the attic can also be a room where the whole family enjoys growing plants and relaxing. A solar attic takes a lot of planning and getting acquainted with new materials, but the rewards are worth the effort. Perhaps the following considerations will help you decide what to do in your attic.

SKYLIGHTS

Before you order a prefabricated skylight, go up into the attic and inspect your insulation. If you have fiberglass or cellulose batting between the rafters, I would suggest that you add aluminum-faced rigid insulation over it. You can fasten the board with special washer-head nails, directly to the rafters. The rigid insulation will help keep in additional heat, as well as provide a reflecting surface that bounces the light around.

The biggest problem you face building your own skylight is making sure it is leak-proof. In most areas, there are prefabricated skylights available which are constructed to eliminate problems of leaking by using a self-flashing system.

Because skylights have been used on industrial buildings for many years, there are many sizes and shapes on the market (Figure 36). Knowing the distance between the rafters in your attic, you can select the proper skylight. Some of these units, advertised as roof windows, are glazed with glass, while skylights are usually rigid plastic. You should select a type that will open easily for summer ventilation.

If you want a large solar growing area, you should consider a continuous arched skylight which might be as long as your roof. You can install a long skylight and not cut any rafters, yet lose very little light. Probably one of the easiest types to install is the ridge panel, but because the winter sun is so low you will get little direct sun.

The best frame is probably the heavy vinyl used in many prefabricated units. Rigid vinyl is tough and is the same color all the way through, so you don't have to worry about painting. Because vinyl is a poor conductor of heat, you avoid the heat loss problems of aluminum.

As for glazing, you can purchase most skylights in double-wall, high impact plastic. You should get one that has a screen insert so that during the summer, when the skylight is open, you are not bothered with insects. If you would rather have glass, then get one of the tilt-out roof windows.

It is difficult to construct skylights so that the glazing angle is perpendicular to the rays of the sun, but you will find that the angle of the average roof facing the equator is close enough to give you good light and heat for growing.

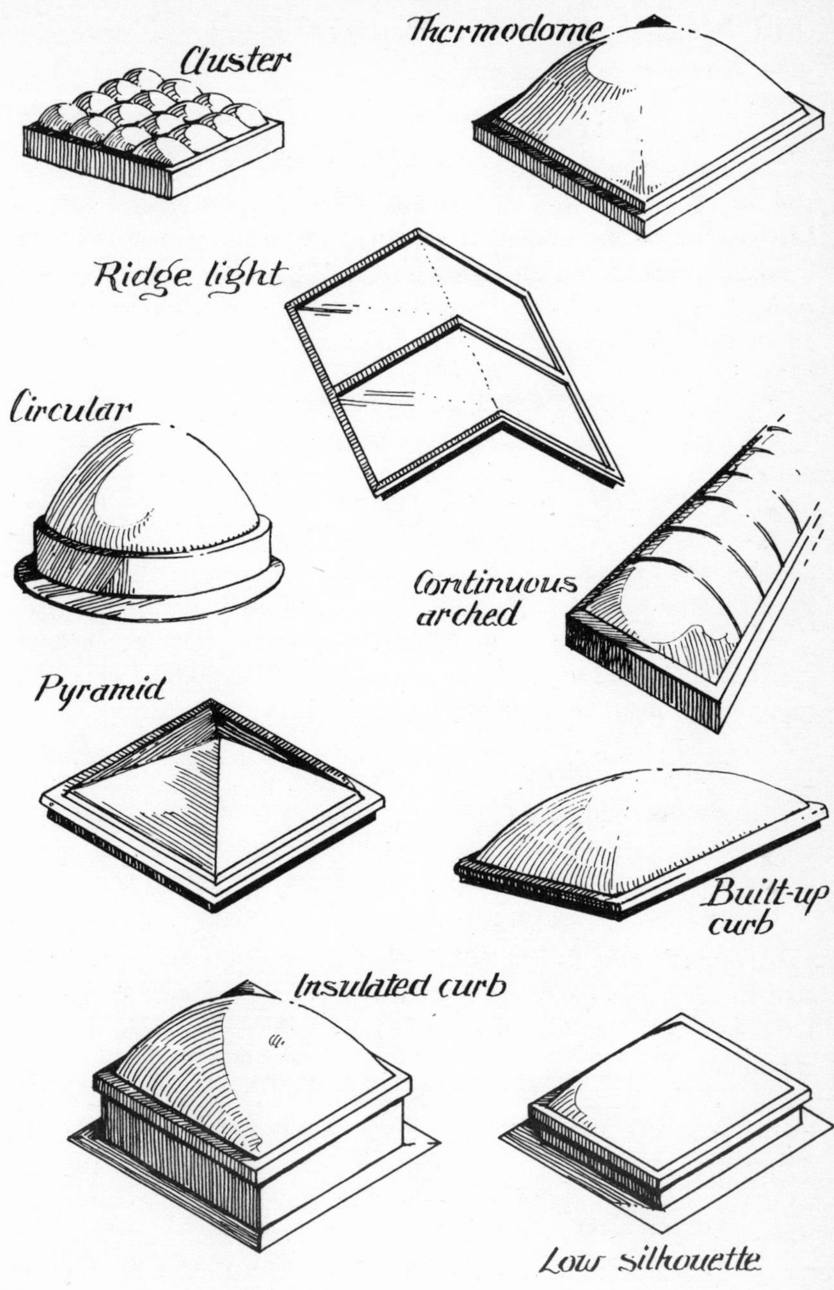

Figure 36. *Various types of skylights.*

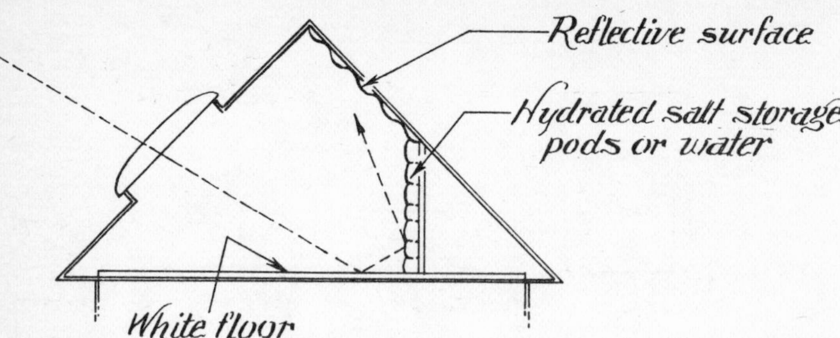

Figure 37. Attic skylight.

ADAPTING FOR SOLAR GROWING

Once the skylight is in, study the light and shadow patterns in the attic and put reflective material in the dark areas so that the light will be spread around. If you can get the light moving around enough, it will bump into storage material and turn to heat (Figure 37). Even places that do not receive direct sunlight will reflect diffuse solar energy and give you heat, so be thorough with the reflective material.

HEAT STORAGE MATERIALS

Rather than trying to cope with heavy containers of water in your attic, I would suggest using hydrated salt phase change pods or rods. Probably the best location would be just below the reflective material on the back wall. For a very attractive floor and additional heat storage as well, try using dark red clay tile about 6 inches (15 cm) or 8 inches (20 cm) square. First, lay a sheet of polyethylene over part of the existing attic floor. Nail a holding strip on three sides using 1 by 3 stained redwood color. Now lay the tiles in dry and tight together. When you reach the third side, nail down the final strip so that all the tile is held securely. The tile will absorb heat and also make a good surface for a solar garden room floor.

GROWING SYSTEMS

As long as you use lightweight soil mixes, you can grow in all kinds of boxes, tubs and hanging baskets. I find it convenient to have tubs on casters so that I can shift the plants around for the best growing conditions. In this setting you might like to try some series-type hanging baskets.

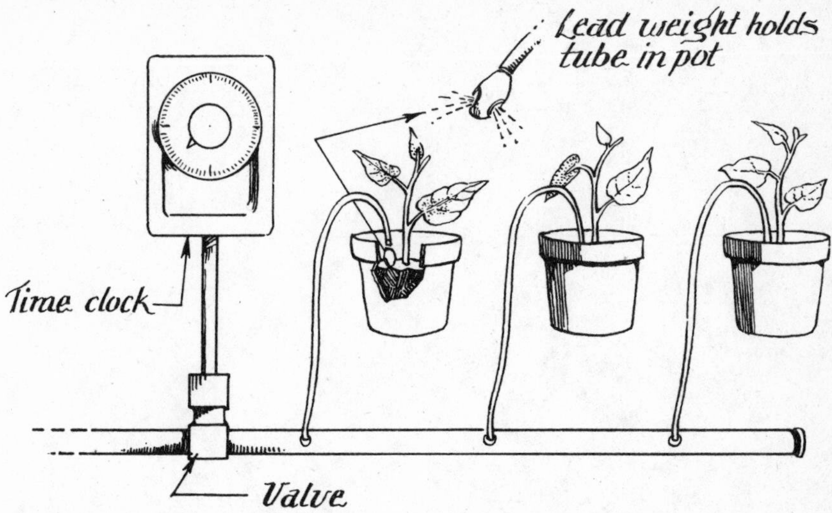

Figure 38. *Spaghetti tube watering.*

For watering, it is best to have a plumber extend a cold water pipe and faucet right into the attic, and if you get so many plants that hand watering becomes a chore, then you can install an automatic spaghetti tube system (Figure 38). I use this system on a time clock which allows me to control the amount of water that is reaching each pot. When you first have the system set up, place one of the spaghetti tubes in a measuring container and see how long it takes to get 4 ounces (125 ml) of water into the container. Then set the time clock for this interval and every time you water, you will get 4 ounces (125 ml) in each pot. This amount is about right for a 6 inch (15 cm) pot. The materials for this type of watering system are available at most greenhouse supply or nursery and garden companies.

HYDROPONICS

If you take a water supply into the attic, then you should consider hydroponic growing. You can buy hydroponic kits that are easily assembled and usually come with complete instructions for care and feeding of the plants (Figure 39). Here are some of the advantages of hydroponic growing.

1. You avoid the mess of dirt on the floor and carrying materials up and down stairs.

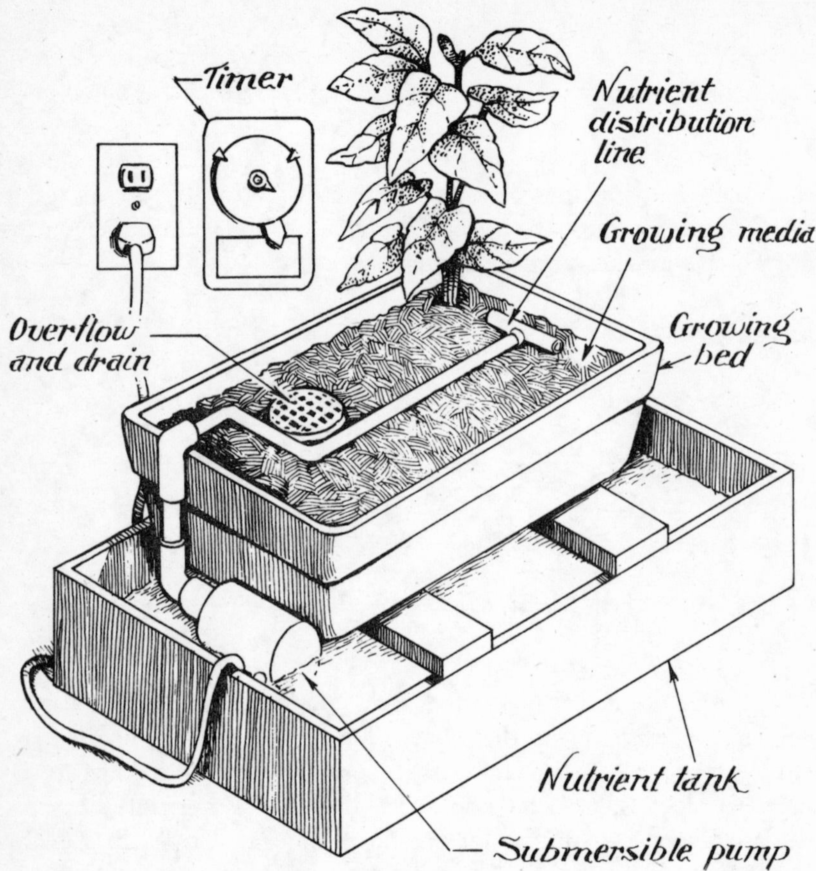

Figure 39. *Automated hydroponic system using wooden box for the nutrient tank and dishpan for the growing bed.*

2. Watering and feeding is easier. You dissolve the fertilizer in the water. Watering is done automatically in sealed compartments which may also act as heat storage material.

3. Less labor is involved because you do not have to weed or cultivate your crops.

4. Yields are often higher. Particularly with some of the food plants like tomatoes and lettuce; you will get four to five times the yield expected in the garden.

5. You have better control. In a solution, it is easier to adjust the relative acidity and the quantity of fertilizer. The response of the plants to the nutrients is much quicker when you feed with liquid fertilizers.

If you plan to do hydroponic gardening in the attic, the sun will provide the heat and light, and hydroponics will furnish the other things you need for good growth. In the Bibliography, you will find references for further information on hydroponics.

VENTILATION

There will be days in the winter when the sun comes out bright and hot and the heat storage materials will keep the attic garden comfortable. The temperature may go up to 90°F (32°C) very rapidly, but it will come down just as fast when the storage materials begin to absorb the heat. In the summer you will probably need an attic exhaust fan on a thermostat to keep temperatures reasonable. If the winter temperatures do climb too high, you can move the heated air down into the house with a duct and fan system. This is another situation where a small turbulator fan in the ceiling, or peak, of the room will circulate warm air down to the heat storage materials.

You can have a lot of fun taking a new look at the attic and the possibilities of converting it to a place where you can grow fresh lettuce and radishes for the evening meal (Figure 40).

DORMER

When you open up the roof to get more light, you want the construction to look architecturally pleasing, and the best way to do this may be with dormer windows. To get the proper angle for sun energy, you can build the dormer to standard construction and then insert the glazing at the correct angle. To get even more light into the solar garden room, you can use reflective materials outside the glazing. When you install dormers, you add stand-up space inside the attic at the window and this may be an advantage.

Providing you do not lose too much energy, it is much simpler to install skylights or skyscopes than to tackle a major construction job. You should consult an architect or builder and compare the costs of different methods of opening up the attic roof in order to come to a practicable solution.

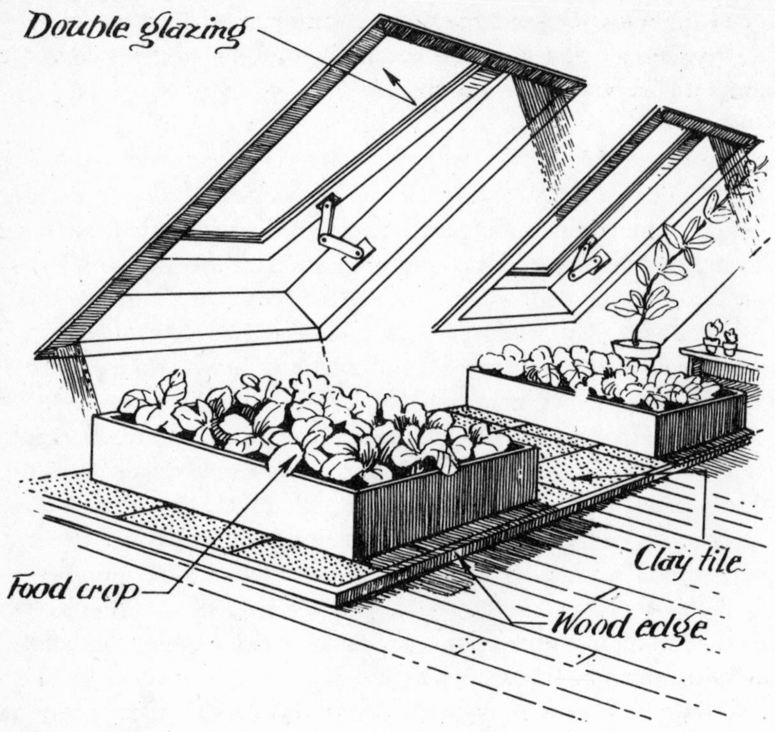

Figure 40. Attic solar garden.

SKYSCOPES

Some ingenious person who wanted a lot of light in the attic, but not a large area of glazing, invented the skyscope. This device consists of a cylindrical, transparent, polycarbonate tube or box, that projects about 30 inches (76 cm) above the roof surface. Inside the tube, there is reflective material angled to reflect light down through two diffusing lenses and into the room. The lenses spread the light around in the attic so that you get a lot of light in through a small opening. There is one model of the skyscope which is a sealed capsule containing a tracking mirror. The mirror follows the sun to give you optimum light in the attic, as long as the sun shines. The tracking model uses small electric motors to keep it constantly angled toward the sun.

The skyscope will help provide enough light for a sizable solar garden in the most forgotten room in the house. As people begin to remodel the house for solar purposes, I can foresee the entire upper storey becoming a glass-enclosed family living room where everyone can luxuriate in the warmth of the sun!

Kitchen

You can have a solar garden in any room where there is enough sunlight. Perhaps you should take inventory of all the rooms on the side of your house facing the equator, and see which are best suited to a solar garden. You may even want to add windows to that room to get more sun energy. Many people spend more time in the kitchen than anywhere else, so let's look at it first.

Many kitchens have a sink facing the sun, and often a window over the sink. This is the ideal place for an herb garden. Box gardens on casters are also convenient because you can move them around to appropriate light conditions. I have even had hanging baskets of lettuce near the sink window.

The kitchen is the obvious place to grow all the winter salad greens and a few tomatoes. The humidity is usually higher than in some other rooms, and during the winter the lights are often on and will provide supplementary energy for plant growth. If you have enough sunlight this is a good room for solar gardening. If not, add wall mirrors to bounce the light around.

Dining Room

We all enjoy the picnic feeling that comes with dining in a garden. This is the place for decorative planters and hangers, plant stands and window boxes for the interior. The scent of orange blossoms or gardenias in flower enhances any meal. Inspect the manner in which restaurants tuck plants in little corners or hang them overhead and still leave room for dining. You can get some good ideas while dining out.

Bathroom

The conditions for growth in the bathroom are excellent, provided there is enough light. The colored tile will absorb solar radiation, humidity is high, temperatures up, and with sunlight you can grow anything. Space is the usual limitation. This is a good place for hanging plants and window sill solar growing (Figure 35).

Living Room

This is the best room for a floor garden and it will create a restful, relaxing atmosphere. Select a sunny location and cover the floor with a waterproof material. In this setting, dark green waterproof outdoor carpeting will blend with the other furnishings and minimize the problems of water spillage. Instead of having the plants in pots, why not have a raised bed garden? Make a wall of brick stacked up dry and line it with a sheet of black polyethylene. Fill this with a mixture of peat and vermiculite, or any other lightweight materials, and then plunge the pots into it so that they appear to be in the ground. You have probably seen this done at flower and garden shows for exhibition purposes and it works just as well in the living room for a permanent garden. Keep the lightweight mix moist, but not soaking wet, and the humidity will be just right for the plants and healthful for you.

We develop trends in the use of plants and a recent one has been to bring plants inside in pots and hangers. Because the light conditions inside are poor, we have limited ourselves to tropical species which will grow with reduced light. Now we are experiencing a trend toward letting more light into the residence, and raised-bed floor gardens are certain to follow, as the new way of enjoying all kinds of plants all year round.

You should consider adding a bay window if space is a problem in your living room. Such a window can add to the architectural charm of the house, as well as increase the resale value.

Bedroom

If you have the best exposure to the sun in a bedroom, there is no reason why you can't adapt it to growing plants. There are, however, some things to consider. If you like to sleep with the window open in the winter, then keeping the plants warm enough is a problem. If you live in a mild climate, or you don't open the windows at night, then temperature is not a problem and you can practise solar growing in the bedroom. Remember that plants take in oxygen and give off carbon dioxide at night, just as people do, so you are really competing with the plants for whatever oxygen supply there is in the room. This is one reason why nurses don't like to have a hospital room overcrowded with too many potted plants.

Utility Room

The utility room is usually a drab little place with washer, dryer and perhaps a furnace. By adding a skylight or window, you might get enough light to grow plants in hangers or on a shelf underneath a skylight.

Almost any room in the house is potentially a solar garden, providing you can let in enough light. You can use mirrors and white walls to move light around inside the room.

If availability permits I would recommend using hydrated salt devices for heat storage. If you use thermal water tubes, place them against a white wall to get the maximum reflection of light on the tubes. Ask your paint supplier which of the white paints has the best reflective qualities, as the more light reflected, the better your plants will grow.

Perhaps the most important factor in using the utility room as a solar grower is an energy-efficient skylight. There are now on the market "insulated" skylights which are very lightweight, even in sizes up to 5 feet (1.5 m) by 20 feet (6.1 m) long. These are made of reinforced, shatter-proof fiberglass in a welded structural aluminum frame. Letting in solar radiation through skylights reduces the cost of heating the house. How pleasant a utility room can be with a large skylight and hanging baskets in which to grow fresh strawberries!

Many of the materials for converting rooms to solar growing are new and may not yet be available where you live. If you have difficulty finding out where to get products, please feel free to write to me for help.

To explore all the possibilities for home solar gardening, you should also take a look at adapting decks, porches, breezeways, entrances, garages and carports.

Deck

A few simple procedures will convert a deck into a solar garden room.

1. Cover the floor of a spaced-wood deck with 5/8 inch (16 mm) tongue-and-groove plywood. On top of this put a layer of rigid insulation board.

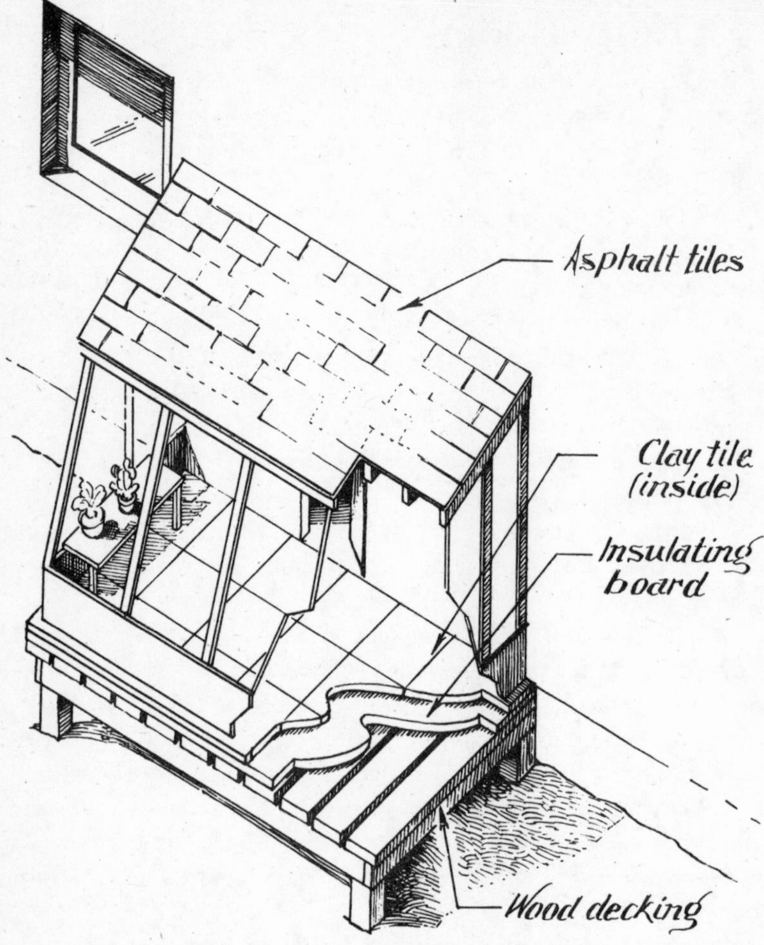

Figure 41. Solar grower on a deck.

2. Framing may be aluminum or wood to match the exterior of the house, double glazed with glass or rigid double-wall plastic sheets.

3. For heat storage, use clay tile on the floor. Against the back wall use either solar pods or solar rods.

4. To keep heat in during the winter and out during the summer, use inflated air blanket curtains on the inside of the solar garden room.

5. At least half of the roof should be standard solid construction to provide shade from the high summer sun. The low winter sun will come in under the solid portion of the roof.

You can arrange growing areas to suit your needs and decorate with outdoor furniture, shelves and hanging plants.

If water and electricity are not available in the deck area, you can extend these services from the house.

In order to enjoy the sun garden deck during the warm summer months, you should provide for shade and ventilation. You might also consider installing glazing panels which can be removed and replaced with screens for summer.

Most decks see limited usage because of bad weather and insects. When you convert your deck to a solar garden room, you'll find that family and friends will enjoy it more often and delight in new experiences such as picking grapes for lunch during a thunderstorm!

Porch

A porch is really a deck with a roof already on it, so that many of the considerations mentioned above also apply.

Should you do something to the porch roof to let in more light? If the porch faces the equator and the roof is high, then you may leave the roof as a solid structure. You should observe the light and shadow patterns on the porch during a winter day. If you think more light would be worthwhile, then you can modify the roof.

This is an instance where flat 5 ounce (140 g) fiberglass is an excellent glazing material. It comes in 4 foot (1.2 m) widths up to 50 feet (15 m) long, allowing you to have continuous glazing over much of the roof without complicated procedures to avoid leaking. The fiberglass should be double glazed to reduce heat loss.

After you have removed the existing roof covering down to the rafters, you can apply the first layer of fiberglass directly to the rafters and the insert purlins (the horizontal rafter supports). Large head aluminum nails will hold the fiberglass securely. Next, nail 3/4 inch (19 mm) spacing boards over all the framing members to keep the two layers of fiberglass apart. When you apply the second layer of fiberglass, make sure that it extends over the existing roofing on the lower edge to take care of water runoff. Install flashing along the top and sides so there will be no leaks. When you are handling fiberglass, be sure to have the

Tedlar-coated side up so that the surface will not be discolored by wind abrasion. One further note about fiberglass. When rain comes down in a torrent, it is very noisy underneath fiberglass. If this is objectionable, I would suggest you glaze with tempered glass.

Besides adapting the roof, you can develop the porch as a solar garden room, much as you would a deck, using heat storage and reflective materials.

Entranceway

Many homes have a landing area at the front door which can be roofed and enclosed to give you a solar garden room. The same methods that you use for decks and porches apply to this situation.

The front entry is the area that gives visitors their first impression of you and your residence. What better first impression than a delightful garden of flowers and fragrance?

The solar entrance garden also has practical advantages. It serves as an air lock to keep sudden cold drafts out of the house and, in cold climates, provides a place to take off winter boots and clothing.

Breezeway

Many people have a garage separated from the house by a walk and roof, commonly called a breezeway. Now that you are beginning to think about places to practise solar gardening, I'm sure you can see that the same principles and methods you use for decks, porches and entryways, can convert your breezeway into a lovely solar garden room (Figure 42).

Garage

You can adapt the garage, or other outbuildings in the same way as the attic or porch to create a solar garden. Usually the garage serves as a storage depot for the car and a host of other family belongings, so there is not very much room left for solar growing. You are probably better off to add an attached solar grower or extend the garage roof and enclose a garden room.

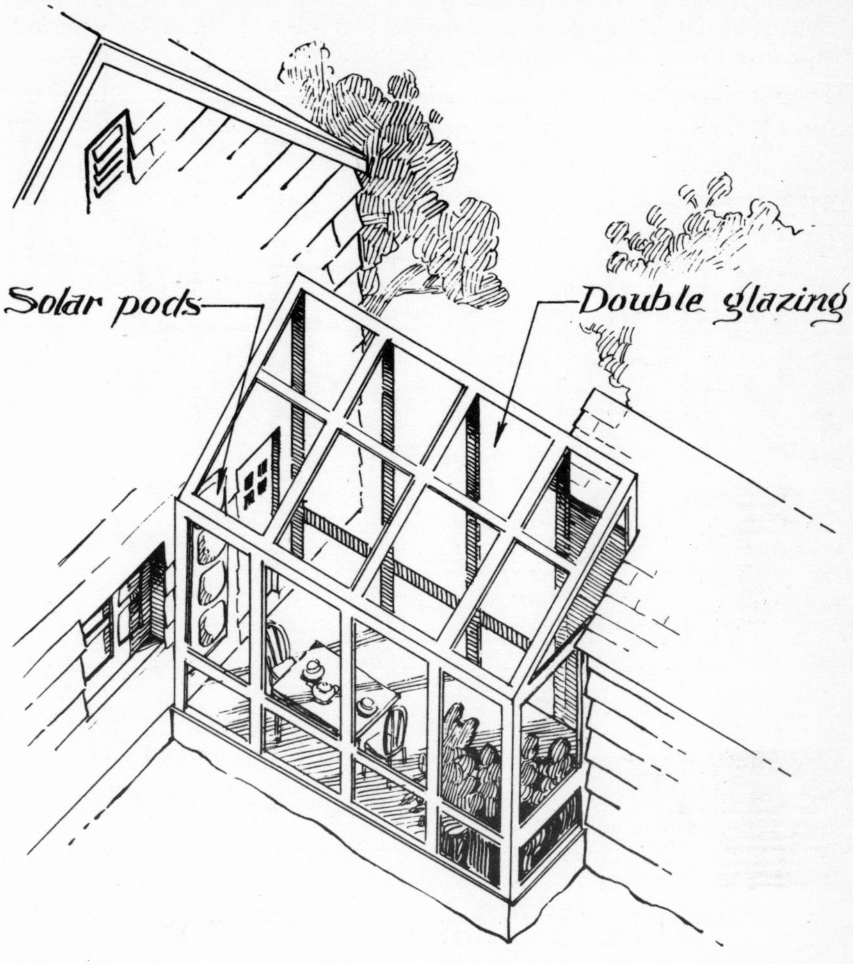

Figure 42. Solar garden breezeway.

If the garage has the best exposure, facing the equator, then you should consider locating the solar grower there to get maximum light for growth. Study the light and shadow patterns around the garage on a sunny winter day, and see what you have for light.

Construction methods are the same as those for the other outside solar garden rooms.

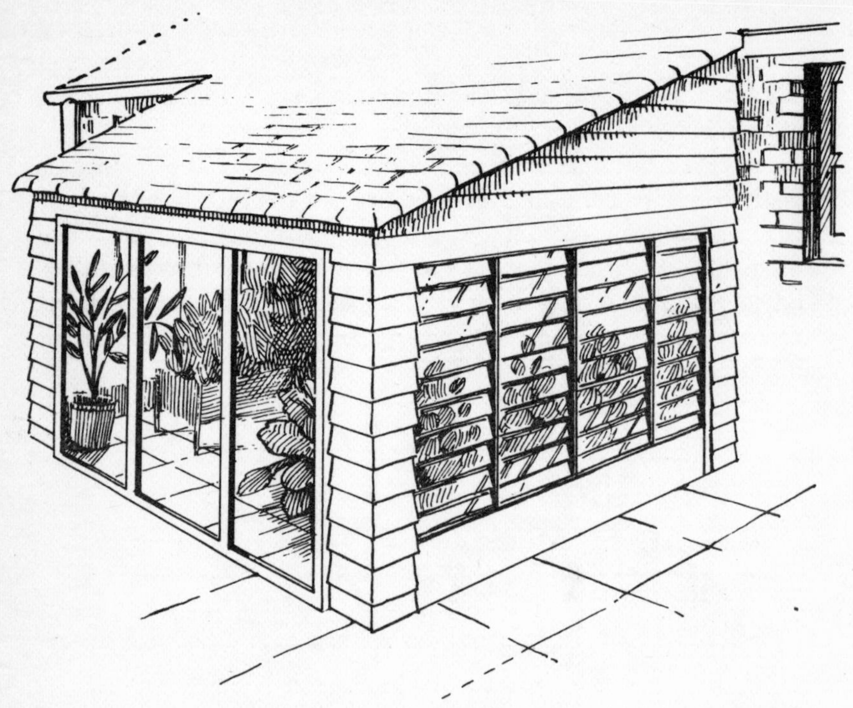

Figure 43. *Add-on solar garden room with tile floor and brick wall for heat absorption. The glazing angle is sacrificed for the sake of appearance.*

Add on a Solar Plant Room

Often the best way get the light you need is to add on a room. You can design the room to be convenient for solar growing and for family relaxation (Figure 43). The usual recreation room is designed for people first. You should design a solar plant room for plants first. Here are some guidelines:

1. Use clay tile, slate or waterproof linoleum for the floor, and if possible, install a drain so that you can take a hose and clean up when necessary.

2. Glaze as much of the wall as possible with double glass both to get light in and to be able to see out, for there is something refreshing about letting your eye run over the landscape. Translucent glazing in this type of plant room would give you the feeling of being in a closet.

3. A skylight or two will give you extra light at the back of the solar plant room where it joins the house. Remember light is the energy which produces growth, so the more light you have, the bigger your plants will be.

4. The furniture for the solar plant room should be painted wrought iron or pressure treated wood to resist the high humidity.

A solar plant room is a wonderful opportunity to create a living space and a solar garden that fits you and your family. Plan carefully, and if you need ideas don't hesitate to consult an architect or builder. Very often the cost of professional help comes back many times in the improved resale value of the dwelling.

Figure 44. *Underground solar grower.*

Chapter 7

NEW CONSTRUCTION SOLAR GARDENS

EXISTING HOMES built before sun awareness began to affect architecture gave little thought to light as an energy source for growing plants in the home. The conventional house was designed as a shelter from the weather and a place to keep warm. What you are considering is a new unified design concept that combines sun-energy architecture with food growing, solar flower gardens and facilities which let you express your particular life-style. To do this requires a different kind of planning.

Planning

First, how much space do you want to devote to food gardening, and how much to other activities? Take inventory of the people involved, and their routines. Do you plan to stay in this residence for a long time or do you move often? You have to ask yourself these questions, and many others, in order to make the space fit your objectives. This type of information will help you design a floor plan, or will assist an architect or builder to make a plan for you.

Consider for a moment the resale value of your present residence ten years from now. There will come a time when older homes that are not designed and constructed to use solar energy for heating and growing will be worth much less than the new energy-efficient houses. This suggests that there is a time to sell or demolish an existing structure, which is decreasing in value, and a time to build a new structure, which will increase in value.

Second, you should have an assessment done of the site on which the new residence is to be located. How does the sun move during the day and during the seasons in relation to your house? How much sun energy per unit area is reaching your land and house? These questions are best answered by a professional solar architect or engineer. When you combine your well-considered objectives with the expertise of a solar professional, you will get a unified design that is far superior to anything you can achieve in the remodeled older home (Figure 45).

Orientation

If you live on a level lot, then you should build the long axis of the house facing the equator so that you can get sun energy into as many rooms as possible. The back side of the house, away from the equator, needs only enough light to be comfortable. Perhaps this side could have no windows at all.

If you live on a hillside, you should consider a partially underground house that snuggles into a slope using earth to reduce heating costs but with window areas exposed to the sun (Figure 44). Here are some of the advantages of the underground structure.

1. Underground or earth-sheltered construction eliminates heat loss due to wind chill and infiltration.

2. The earth tends to even out temperature swings and gives constant, even warmth.

3. Although underground construction may cost as much as 20 percent more than conventional building methods, the savings in heating costs more than offset the increase.

4. Underground homes cost less to heat. If the ground outside is 45°F (7°C), the air is 0°F (−18°C), and you want to keep the inside temperature at 65°F (18°C), then the earth-sheltered structure only has to provide a heat rise of 20°F (11°C) higher than its surroundings while the conventional structure must raise the temperature 65°F (36°C)

Figure 45. Solar house.

higher. This means a substantial saving in the cost of heating the earth-sheltered structure.

References in the Bibliography will give you further information on underground structures. Before you decide not to build an earth-sheltered home, you should read the literature on underground architecture and see how you feel about this new development. If you are purchasing land, look for a site that lends itself to optimum use of solar energy. If you cannot site the house directly toward the equator, then an angle to the east will give you the best heat and light energy.

Glazing

You can construct your house with the correct glazing angle for the entire side of the structure that faces the equator. Where you want to be able to see out, use double glass, and where you want privacy, use Heliolite prismed glass or polycarbonate sheet.

Remember that you are trying to get as much light and heat as possible into your home, so you use solid walls on the sides and make the sun side all glazing. You can use long-handled extension poles to wash the glazing periodically. It is a good idea to use tempered glass to avoid the problems of replacing broken glass.

Thermopane glass is hermetically sealed at the factory and this solves the problem of condensation, but it is also very expensive for the large expanses that you want in a sun energy house. You can use double layers of tempered glass about 1/2 inch (13 mm) apart. When you add an outer layer of glass, the temperature of the inner layer rises by about 15°F (9°C), and the heat loss through the window is reduced 50 percent. During the winter, the outside air is drier than the air inside the house which carries the moisture from cooking and baths, so you have to seal the glass thoroughly. If warm, humid air from the house leaks between the layers of glass, you get condensation. The best solution for this situation is to drill small weep holes through the frame to the outside. This tends to keep the air between the layers of glass at about the same humidity level as the outside air and you get less condensation.

Aesthetics

For your personal satisfaction and to keep its resale value up, the structure should be attractive on the outside. I would suggest that you collect pictures and take photographs of sun houses that you like. You can give these pictures to the architect or builder to help him arrive at a suitable design for your own residence.

Interiors

Everyone wants a house of his or her own, but with the price of new construction rising every year, it seems less and less possible for many. Perhaps the answer lies in a new solar house that lets you save money on heating and provides space enough for solar gardens to reduce the food bill. Over a period of years, lowering the cost of food and heat can add up to substantial savings.

This means adjusting your life-style to new activities, such as tending the solar garden, composting kitchen waste and washing large expanses of glass. If it is the means of helping you afford a house of your own, it is worth the adjustments required.

Let's look at how some people deal with their solar growers.

In Figure 46, you can see a solar garden in a raised bed and in large tubs. The light comes through the double glazing and is absorbed

Figure 46. Deep bed solar gardening.

by the brick walls and the tile floor. The planting bed is deep enough for such crops as asparagus and rhubarb. There is plenty of room for tropical palms, fig trees or any other large plants that suit your fancy.

Behind the double glazing in Figure 47 is a swimming pool and planting area. The water acts as heat storage material and a reflective surface. The planting area is large enough for a good crop of food plants. The open water also provides humidity for good plant growth.

During the hours that you spend in the kitchen, you can have the green feeling of a solar garden. A planting bed in an extended window is deep enough for salad greens and all the herbs you will want for gourmet cooking.

Figure 47. Sun-heated indoor pool and garden.

If your dining space is large enough, you can combine different activities, including solar gardening, in one area. White walls will reflect light onto a tile floor for heat absorption.

If you are the first to build a sun energy house in your area, it will look different than the other houses in the neighborhood. But as more energy efficient houses are built, the old conventional house will be the oddity.

If you are planning to buy a house, then you will want to visit housing developments of dwellings that make use of the sun energy. Somewhere in your area you will find a chapter of the International Solar Energy Society and they can direct you to the nearest sun houses. Once you walk around inside one of these houses and see how it feels to live and grow in the sun, you'll never be happy living in a big closet with windows.

Figure 48. Dining in the solar garden.

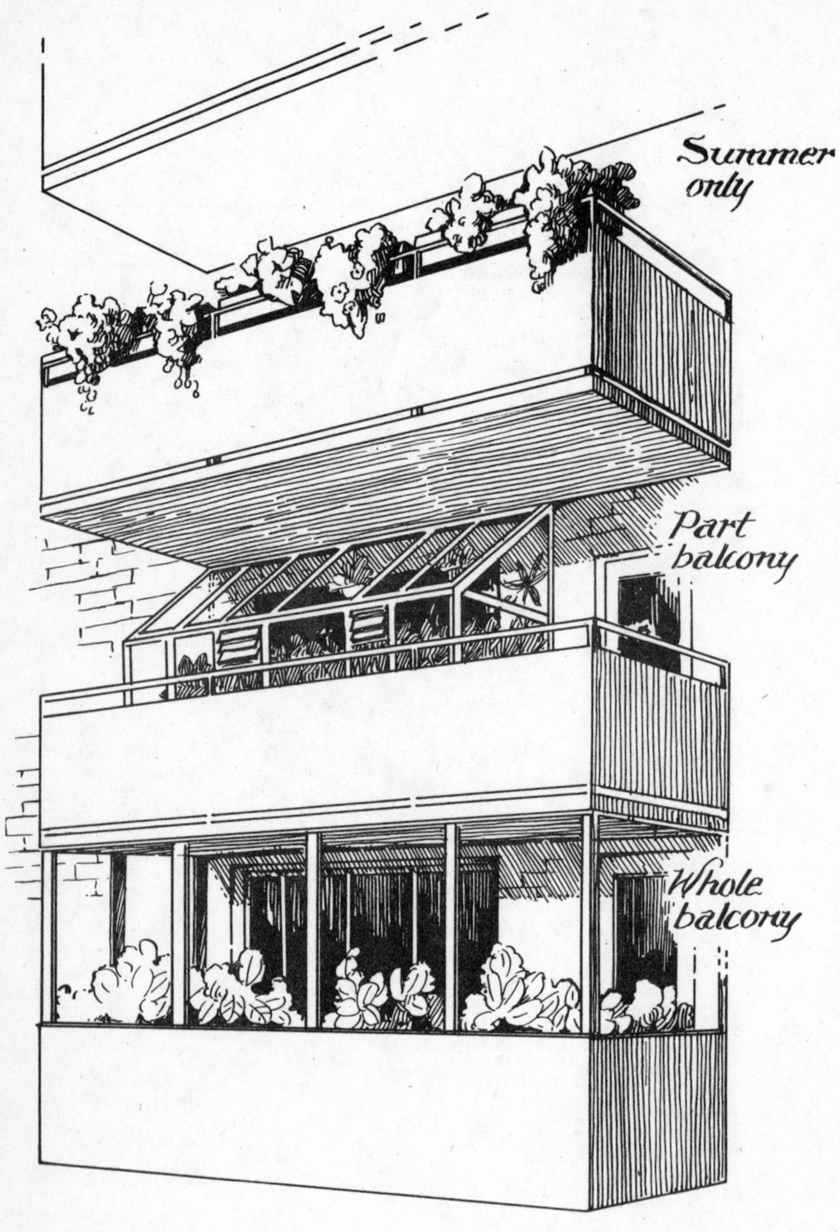

Figure 49. Balcony solar growing.

Chapter 8

APARTMENT SOLAR GROWING

YOU CAN ENJOY the pleasures of solar gardening on a balcony, whether it is on a private home, a suburban flat or on the seventeenth floor of a city high-rise.

You Own the Balcony

The best procedure for a balcony you own is to enclose the entire area and create an extra solar garden room.

ORIENTATION

You can't move a balcony around to get more sun energy, but you can enhance the natural light by using as much reflective surface as possible. You can use foil or aluminized mylar on the back wall, which will give you direct beam reflection onto the heat storage material, or you can paint the wall white, which gives you diffused light.

Light provides the energy for growth, so there may well be limitations to what you can grow on a shaded balcony. Borrow a light meter and see how much light you have on your balcony. If you have less than 500 foot-candles, I would suggest that you do your food gardening elsewhere, but with this light intensity, you can still grow a wide variety of tropical foliage plants for decoration. The alternative is to add supplementary light. Cool white fluorescent lamps with one or two incandescent bulbs will give you the light spectrum you need for growth, and enough light intensity to grow all the food plants.

GLAZING

The primary consideration on a balcony is weight. The lightest glazing is polycarbonate or acrylic double-wall sheeting. At the same time, these materials are very strong. Manufacturers test the strength of the sheeting by swinging a 5 pound (2.2 kg) ball at a surface from 40 feet (12 m) away. This is an impact of 200 foot pounds and yet the sheeting will not break! The sheets come 4 feet (1.2 m) wide and up to 24 feet (7 m) long, so you can have them cut to fit your particular situation. Light transmittance is 90 percent of what you get with glass.

The lightest framing material is aluminum, and there are some greenhouse supply companies that carry aluminum framing made to receive 5/8 inch (16 mm) rigid plastic as glazing. You can have the framing cut and drilled to assemble yourself, or you can have it done by a greenhouse contractor. If your balcony will support the weight, you can use a wood frame painted or stained to match the siding on the building. Using rigid plastic panels that are 4 feet (1.2 m) wide means less framing weight than glass glazing, which is commonly installed in 2 foot (.6 m) widths. If you want to use double glass glazing, then you can support the balcony with braces to carry the extra weight.

HEAT STORAGE

Probably the best heat storage material for this situation is hydrated salts. You can use clay tile on the floor, and rods, panels or solar tiles on the back wall. If the floor of the balcony is spaced lumber, like a deck, then I would suggest that you cover the wood with a layer of polyethylene, or apply a solid plywood surface over the open decking. On top of the plywood, put a layer of aluminized building paper and then set the tiles down dry, without mortar and as close together as you can.

If you live in a cold climate and need more heat for good winter growth, you can always open a window or door into the house or apartment and let the warm air circulate. By the same token, if the temperature gets too high in the balcony grower, you can let the warm air into the dwelling. As long as you have electricity readily available in the house or apartment, you can use a thermostat to operate a kitchen exhaust fan installed in the wall to accomplish the heat transfer.

The best method of retaining winter heat in the balcony solar grower is the inflated air blanket, discussed previously. In very warm areas, you might want to leave the air blanket up all summer for insulation against the hot summer sun.

You Rent the Balcony

Of course, you have to talk to the owner or manager of the building before you do anything. Before you talk, plan what you want to do and, if possible, locate some people with balcony growers that will let you bring the owner in to see what they have done. In many cities, there are organizations of people who do hobby gardening above the ground, and they can be of considerable help. You have at least two options for solar growing on a rented balcony: first, to enclose the entire balcony, and second, to put a small prefabricated structure on the balcony (Figure 49).

Enclosing the whole rented balcony is really a job for professionals. The owner may prefer to have the work done himself, or if he gives you permission, you can have a solar contractor do the job for you. In either case, the methods are the same as those for a privately owned balcony.

You may want to buy a prefabricated structure such as a small free-standing greenhouse, a reach-in greenhouse or a frame, and place it on the balcony. You can then adapt this structure for solar growing using the methods already presented for getting the light in, absorbing the heat and keeping the heat in. Certainly this is the quickest and easiest way to get started practising solar growing and if you bolt the structure together, you can take it apart and use it in another place when you move.

Window Gardens

In many parts of the world, houses and apartments are built with very narrow window sills. In order to do solar growing on the window sill, you have to make it wider by putting brackets on the wall immediately under the sill to support a shelf board flush with the sill (Figure 50). This will give you a new window sill about 16 inches wide (40 cm). You can also make the sill addition wider than the window

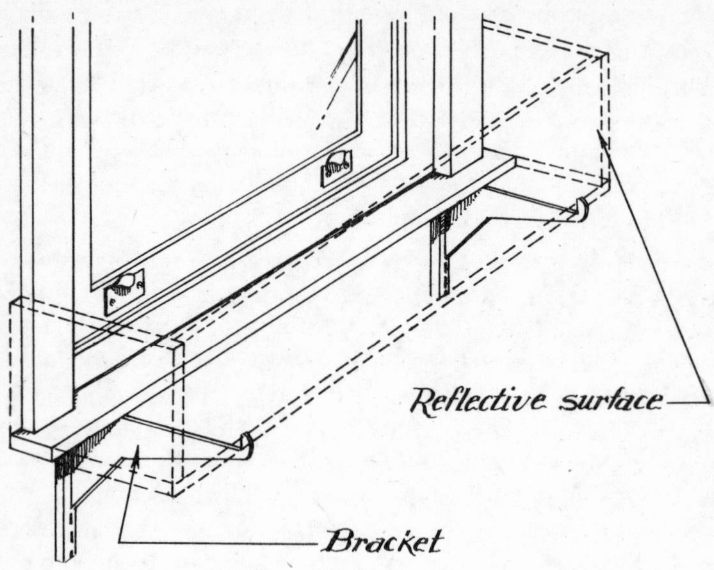

Figure 50. Extending the window sill.

and use reflectors at the ends of the new shelf board. Perhaps you don't have a balcony and need the maximum growth area at your window. In this case, I would suggest a plant stand with several shelf levels, one of which is the window sill. In this way, you can have at least three shelves for plants. In many areas you can buy glass shelves that hang from the top of the window and rest against the pane. These are usually quite narrow but will do for small plants.

Two problems with window sill gardening are the sudden changes in temperature and the humidity. To level out the temperature extremes and also absorb sun heat, I have used clay pots painted black with the plant in a plastic pot placed inside the clay pot. The clay pot absorbs the heat, but with an air space between it and the plastic pot, you will not burn the root system. To improve the humidity, put open saucers of gravel filled with water on the floor below the plant shelves. The water will evaporate and provide moist air for the plants above. For watering, you can buy a small diameter plastic tube watering device which fastens to the kitchen faucet. I have one 50 feet (15 m) long that reaches all the plants in the house from either the bathroom or the kitchen.

You can also hang planters from the ceiling or from wall brackets fastened to the window frame. If you have a spare table, simply place it in front of the window as a plant shelf. To avoid damaging the table, cover it with black polyethylene or linoleum cloth.

Roof Gardens

Every time I stay in a big city hotel I look out the windows at acres of black, empty roof tops, dirty chimneys and air conditioners. I have a landscape architect friend in New York City who is slowly converting these barren elevated spaces into beautiful, productive gardens. You can do this too!

Of course, in an apartment you will have to talk to the building owner and get permission, but it is very practicable. Maybe the owner would like to build a community solar grower on the back of the building for the occupants to use. How can you lose?

MATERIALS

You can build almost any type of solar grower structure on the roof: greenhouse, cold frame, hot bed or super cloche, as long as you use light-weight materials. Check with the owner and find out how much weight the roof will hold. In many areas the building codes specify 60 pounds (27 kg) per square foot (.09 m^2) maximum. Water weighs 62 pounds (28 kg) per cubic foot (.03 m^3) and ordinary soil about 80 to 100 pounds (36 kg to 45 kg) per square foot. You can conform to the weight restrictions by using the lightweight mixes of peat, perlite and vermiculite which give a mix weighing about 34 pounds (15 kg) per cubic foot. Keep your solar grower structure close to the edges of the roof where the supporting structure is strongest.

For framing materials, I would suggest aluminum or soft wood because they are light. The lightest glazing material, that is good for retaining solar heat, is double-wall polycarbonate sheeting, which weighs as little as 4 ounces (125 g) per square foot (.09 m^2).

HEAT ABSORPTION

Most city roofs are black tar and gravel and act as good absorbers of sun heat. The roof will absorb the heat all day, and at night will give you a warmer environment for your solar structure than one on the ground. This means that you need less heat storage material inside the solar grower. There is no lightweight material that absorbs a lot of heat, because the capacity to hold heat is a function of the density of the material. Again, this would be a good place to try hydrated salts in a factory-sealed container since this would give the most heat absorption for the least weight. Otherwise you can use water in containers, as long as you don't exceed the 60 pounds (27 kg) per square foot (.09 m^2), or whatever weight the building codes state.

WIND

You get higher wind velocities on a roof, and in many cities there is also a tunneling effect which increases the wind speed. The glazed solar grower gives you wind protection at any time of year. Make certain that the solar grower is well anchored, by mounting the structure on planks fastened to the roof.

POLLUTION

The increased amount of pollution in the city is both good and bad for plants. It is good because carbon dioxide from the streets below rises and gives roof-top plants more than they would get on the ground. You may remember that plants "breathe in" carbon dioxide and give off oxygen during the day. Unfortunately, when the air rises from the street it also contains other pollutants, including a lot of dust or soot, that will damage plants. A small fan in your solar grower will help reduce the damage from pollution. You will have to wash off the surface of the glazing often to make sure you get all the light possible.

CONTAINERS

Probably the lightest container is a black plastic bag full of a light mix. Ordinary garbage bags work very well. Being black, the bags also act as heat absorption material.

There are lightweight aggregate containers on the market, some of which are very decorative. Perhaps you can find, or have made to your specifications, containers made of hypertufa. This is a mix of one part cement, one part perlite and vermiculite in equal proportions, and two parts milled peat moss. This gives you a light container in just the size and shape you wish.

Community Solar Growing

In many parts of the world, you will find solar grower greenhouses attached to schools, retirement homes and apartment houses.

There are many factories which have solar growing facilities attached to the building so that the workers can spend a lunch period working with plants that they can subsequently take home. In many cities, you can now rent space in a greenhouse built especially for the people who want to garden and do not have room enough at home. Many towns, cities and governmental agencies are providing land that you can rent, either to grow plants in the ground or to erect a solar grower structure. Riding through Europe on the train, you will notice the geometric pattern of little plots of ground on the outskirts of town. Here, people erect a solar shed and spend their weekends year round enjoying the pleasures of gardening and the company of fellow gardeners.

Figure 51. *Black container heat storage in a cold frame.*

Chapter 9

SOLAR FRAMES AND BOXES

MANY GARDENERS who cannot afford the luxury of a walk-in solar grower start with a cold frame because it is very inexpensive to buy or build. The principal problem with a cold frame is the inconvenience. When the snow is blowing and it is bitter cold, you have to be a real plant enthusiast to overcome the inertia required to bundle up in winter clothes and go out to see how the lettuce is doing.

What Is a Frame?

A growing frame is a permanent glazed box used to extend the season in cool or cold climates. Sometimes the box is heated and called a hot bed and sometimes there is no heat provided and it is known as a cold frame.

There is nothing new about growing in a frame. What is new is designing the frame to take maximum advantage of sun heat so that it becomes a solar grower.

FRAME MATERIALS

You can buy prefabricated frames made of wood or aluminum. Aluminum frames lose heat to the air by conduction, and since your objective is to conserve as much heat as possible, the wood frame is better. To avoid the problem of rot, use cedar, yellow wood, eucalyptus, redwood or pressure-treated lumber, as you would if building a larger solar grower. If you treat your own lumber, be sure to use a wood preservative which will not damage plants. Stay away from products containing toxic compounds. Instead, use a product made from copper or zinc naphthenate which stops or prevents rot and decay caused by fungi.

One of the best ways to build your own frame is to find some old glazed windows and build the frame to fit them.

GLAZING MATERIALS

Traditionally, most frames have a single glazing of glass or other material. For the solar grower frame you should double glaze with any of the following materials.

Glass is still the best glazing material for solar growing. Thermopane is really too expensive for a simple structure such as a frame, so I would use a sheet of tempered glass over a sheet of regular double-strength glass. You will get some condensation between the layers of glass, but a frame heats up so rapidly that the condensation will soon dissipate.

You can glaze with flat, 5 ounce (140 g) fiberglass, or plastic or polyethylene. The best material is double-wall acrylic or polycarbonate sheet. If you are using old windows, you should cover them with polyethylene to get the heat saving benefits of double glazing. You can stretch the polyethylene over the frame cover, staple it, then apply nailing strips over the staples.

SIZE

You can make a frame as long as you wish, but keep the width to 3 feet (1 m). This is a comfortable depth to reach in and work with the plants. The height is strictly a matter of what you grow in the frame. Usually the back is about 3 feet (1 m) high and the front about 1 foot (.3 m) high. This is the traditional cold frame. However, to get maximum use of sun energy, this is a poor arrangement. The glazing

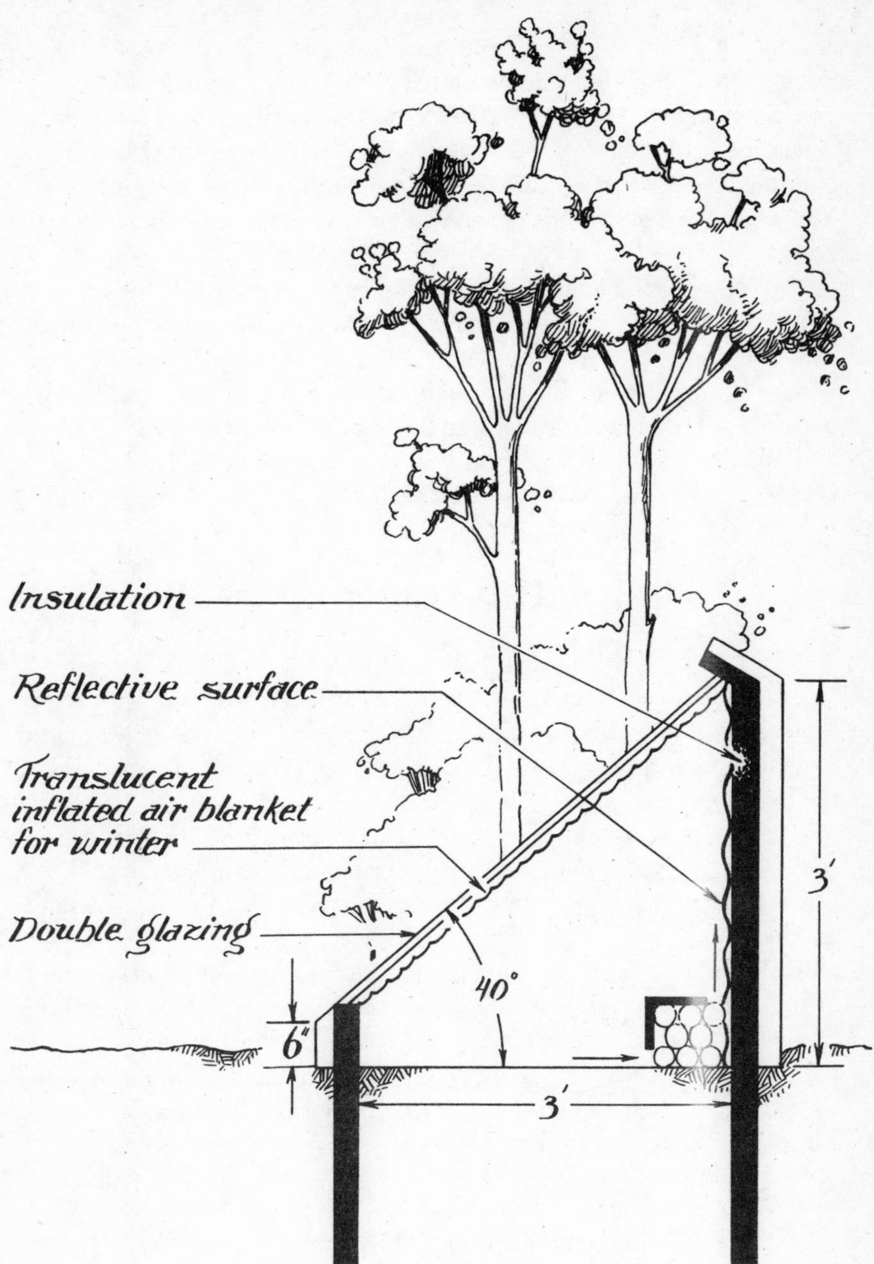

Figure 52. A solar frame for latitude 30°.

angle should be your latitude plus ten degrees. In order to achieve a steep angle in high latitudes, you may well find it advisable to use a partial solid roof. Up to now, the manufacturers have not considered designing a cold frame for solar growing, so you are probably better off building your own to get maximum sun energy into the structure. The reward you get is nice crisp salad greens all winter with no heat costs.

If you build your frame in modules of 6 feet (2 m), then you can line up several in a long row facing the equator and do different things in each unit.

You will see cold frames built like an A-frame with glazing on both the side facing the equator and the side away from the equator. This means one side is functioning as a good solar grower and the other side is not. The back wall, away from the equator, should be vertical.

Adapting the Frame for Solar Growing

Whatever the shape or size of the solar grower, you want to get as much heat and light as possible into the structure; you want to put as much heat absorption material inside as you can; and you want to keep the heat in as long as possible.

If your solar frame cover is at the proper angle, it will shed snow. If snow does accumulate, then remove it by hand and, in general, keep the glazing surface as clean as possible. To keep the light and heat bouncing around inside the grower, I would suggest painting all the interior surfaces with an exterior quality high gloss white enamel, or lining the back wall with aluminum foil. Remember that reflecting the light in this fashion can add as much as one third more heat and light to the structure. Try to avoid placing the solar frame where it is shaded by buildings or trees. Even though trees have no leaves in the winter, the shadow pattern of a tree on your solar frame will greatly reduce the input of light and heat.

HEAT ABSORPTION MATERIALS

The space in a frame solar grower is limited and you want as much area for growing as possible. This suggests that perhaps the best idea for storage is the solar pillow. You can fill black plastic bags with water that are the right size to put between plants, along the sides or on the ground at the base of the back wall. A twisted wire seal is not absolutely water tight, but with the bag partially full there is no internal pressure to cause leaking. If there is some seepage, it will water the plants. Any black containers full of water will store heat and you may want to build your solar frame large enough to accommodate storage other than the solar pillows (see Figure 51). Dark rocks, or black-painted rocks, will absorb more heat than light-coloured stones. I have also used old hard-burned bricks stacked along the walls and in between the plants and hydrated salt containers.

KEEPING THE HEAT IN

Holding the heat in begins with proper insulation. Ideally, the perimeter of the frame should have vertical insulation down to the frostline. You can dig a trench, put in rigid insulation board cut to size and then backfill with earth. If you do not do this, you'll lose a lot of heat by conduction to the cold ground around the frame. I use a rigid polyurethane board with aluminum facing on both sides, fastened to the inside of the box. Wood has very little capacity to absorb and store heat, so you are not losing heat storage capacity when you insulate inside. The insulating board is only an inch (2.5 cm) thick, so you are not losing space for plants.

You can make a night covering for the lid of the frame with the same insulating board. A frame is so small that it gains and loses heat rapidly, thus it is important to lower the night covering as soon as the sun goes down to save all the heat possible.

If you can locate the solar frame so that the back wall is against the house you will find it more convenient to service. In addition, the frame will lose less heat. Again, because a frame is so small, even a short exposure to cold winter winds will take all the heat you have collected during the day, in a very short time.

VENTILATION

A solar frame heats up as quickly as it cools and can easily burn tender foliage on a bright sunny day in the winter. The solution to this problem is easier than keeping heat in. A thermal piston installed on the lid will open as the temperature rises and cool the frame. Some of these thermal piston devices are set at the factory for approximately 80°F (27°C), while others are adjustable. I prefer the adjustable type so that if you are growing crops that require high heat you can set the piston to open at 90°F (32°C). If you are growing a cool crop, like lettuce, you can set the piston to open at 60°F (15°C). Solar growing is letting the sun work for you, in as many ways as possible!

Hot Beds or Heated Frames

It may well be that you cannot get enough sun heat into the solar grower to provide temperatures as high as you want. In this case you should use supplemental heat.

The traditional answer to a source of heat for the hot bed has been manure. If you live in a rural area where horse manure is available, this may be feasible. Fairly fresh manure with about one-third litter is best. A week or so before you plan to put the manure into your grower, pile it up outside like a compost pile and water it until it is moist. Let it stand for at least a week until the center of the pile begins to heat. Your excavation in the grower should be about 2 feet (.6 m) deep. Place the manure in the grower in 6 inch (15 cm) layers, tamping each layer down tight. Leave it with the cover of the frame open for a few days, then cover it with at least 6 to 8 inches (15 to 20 cm) of good loam soil. Now you are ready to plant!

It is most important to use a thermal piston for ventilation when the heat source is a combination of solar and manure. With two heat sources, neither of which can be regulated by a thermostat, you can get sudden increases in temperature which will burn young seedlings. The only means you have of regulating temperature is by ventilating, and you might as well let the sun or the manure heat do it; otherwise, you have to open and close the cover by hand.

There is another alternative if you can get electricity to the grower, and that is a heat cable. Excavate down about 1 foot (.3 m) inside the frame, and pile the soil up outside. Put about 3 inches (8 cm) of perlite, vermiculite or small gravel in the bottom of the excavation. Cover this with 1 inch (2.5 cm) of sand spread out evenly with a board. Now, lay the cable out on the sand as indicated in the drawing that comes with the cable. Cover the cable with an inch of sand, and on top of this place a wire mesh to prevent damaging the cable if you dig in the soil. Over the wire mesh put 6 to 8 inches (15 to 20 cm) of good garden loam or soil and compost. Now fasten the thermostat to the side wall of the frame and connect it to the electricity. The thermostat is usually set for 70°F (21°C) and again with two heat sources, don't forget to use a thermal piston on the lid.

Figure 53. A super cloche with sections raised for ventilation.

Chapter 10

SOLAR CLOCHES AND CROP SHELTERS

THE CLOCHE originated in France as a bell-shaped glass jar used to cover tender young seedlings. The English expanded this idea to include all kinds of covers to protect plants from the cold or the pelting rain.

Types of Cloches

You can now buy cloches of all shapes and sizes made from a variety of transparent and translucent materials (Figure 54). Most of these are widely available in garden shops and nurseries.

Glass cloches come in small panes with a wire clip to hold the pieces together in an A-frame shape over the plants. Glass has the best light transmission ability but breaks easily, unless you use tempered glass. To my knowledge, there are no prefabricated double-glazed glass cloches on the market.

Fiberglass is widely used, especially for tunnel cloches, because it comes in lengths up to 24 feet (7 m). You bend the whole sheet into an arc over the row of plants and hold it in place with a wire retainer.

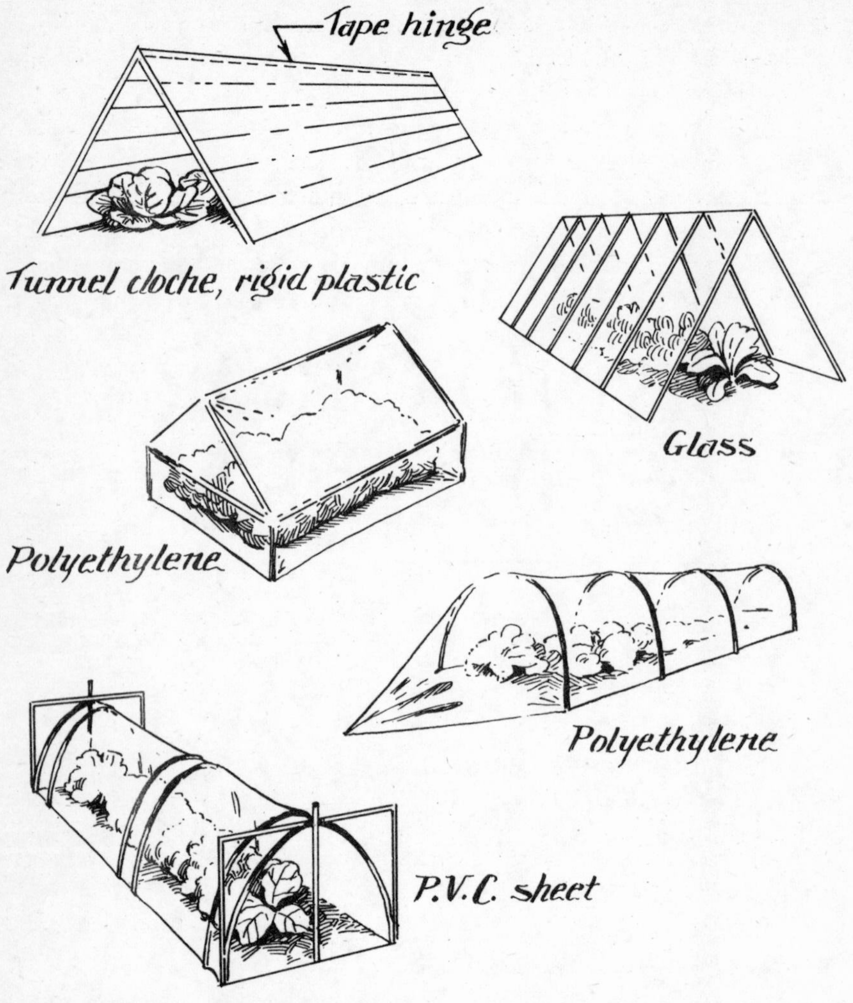

Figure 54. *Various types of cloches.*

Fiberglass is a plastic resin impregnated with glass fibers. It is translucent and admits good light for growth but there is no easy way to double glaze with fiberglass.

Double-wall plastics are probably the best materials for cloches because they admit almost as much light as glass, and hold heat in the growing area better than any single glazing. The materials are polycarbonate, acrylic and polypropylene sheeting. The first two cut easily with a saw and can be fastened like glass to form an A-frame cover.

Polypropylene is softer and more flexible, cuts easily with a knife and diffuses the light. You can bend a long sheet of polypropylene, just like fiberglass, to form a double-glazed tunnel cloche.

Plain polyethylene sheeting can be used over wire frames, but is difficult to double glaze. In addition, heat escapes through polyethylene during the night. There is a polyethylene material bonded to wire mesh which you can bend into any shape that you wish. This material could be used double for better heat retention. However, polyethylene breaks down and must be replaced every three or four years, even when it has been treated to resist ultraviolet light.

For individual plants, you can buy cloches made of wax paper or plastic, variously called hotkaps, sunhats or cap cloches. There is considerable merit in using a tunnel cloche to cover a row of plants and warm the entire growing area.

Solar Mulch

Mulching the outdoor garden is an old familiar practice. Solar mulching is a new way!

1. Prepare your garden area by spading or rototilling several weeks before you want to plant.
2. Spread a layer of black plastic out over the area and hold it down with rocks.
3. The black plastic absorbs sun heat, causing the temperature of the ground underneath to rise several degrees. This means that seed will germinate faster and seedlings will develop more rapidly.
4. Remove the black plastic when you seed, and cut it in strips to use as a solar mulch between the rows.
5. When the plants are up you can change to a different type of mulch, such as grass clippings, straw or peat moss.
6. Put the strips of black plastic back over the organic mulch to conserve heat and accelerate composting.

Solar mulching will give you mature flowers or vegetables much earlier than usual, and at the same time greatly increase your yield.

Crop Shelters or Super Cloches

If you start with a small cloche to cover a single plant, or row of plants, it won't be long before you will want to try one a little larger to cover two or three rows. Eventually you may consider the feasibility of covering the whole garden with a temporary crop shelter or super cloche. The alternative to a collection of small pieces of covering scattered over the garden is one large removable structure that not only lets you extend the season, but may well permit growing all winter with help from the sun.

If you have a large family and plan to do serious food growing, then you can make the crop shelter large enough to grow all the food you need.

PIPE FRAME AND POLYETHYLENE

A simple crop shelter is a pipe frame covered with double-layer inflated polyethylene such as is commonly used to protect nursery stock for the winter. In many places, you can buy a prefabricated frame, which can be readily assembled at home. Most of these come in widths of 22 to 24 (6.7 to 7.3 m) feet and in lengths as long as you wish. For a family of four, a crop shelter 22 feet (6.7 m) wide and 24 feet (7.3 m) long will provide space enough to grow all your vegetable food needs and some flowers too! If you buy a prefabricated frame, the supplier can also sell you polyethylene for a covering along with the necessary equipment and instructions for installation.

Building Your Own Crop Shelter

FRAMING

I like to use 1 inch (2.5 cm) polyvinyl chloride pipe (PVC) for framing material, and treated lumber for the base. The PVC pipe comes in 20 foot (6 m) lengths, which are easy to bend into a smooth curving arch. You can use galvanized pipe or electrical conduit if you build a jig to bend the pipe so that the arches have a uniform curve.

Using one 20 foot (6 m) length of PVC pipe for each arch gives you a structure 12 feet (3.6 m) wide, 7 feet (2.1 m) high at the ridge and as long as you want to make it to get the growing room that you need. The procedure for construction is as follows:

1. Stand 2 by 10 boards on edge for the length of one side of the shelter and stake them in an upright position.

2. Fasten a 20 foot (6 m) length of pipe to the inside of the 2 by 10 base, using pipe strap fastened with screws (Figure 55).

3. Measure 12 feet (3.6 m) for the width, stand on edge and stake a second row of 2 by 10 lumber as a base for the other side.

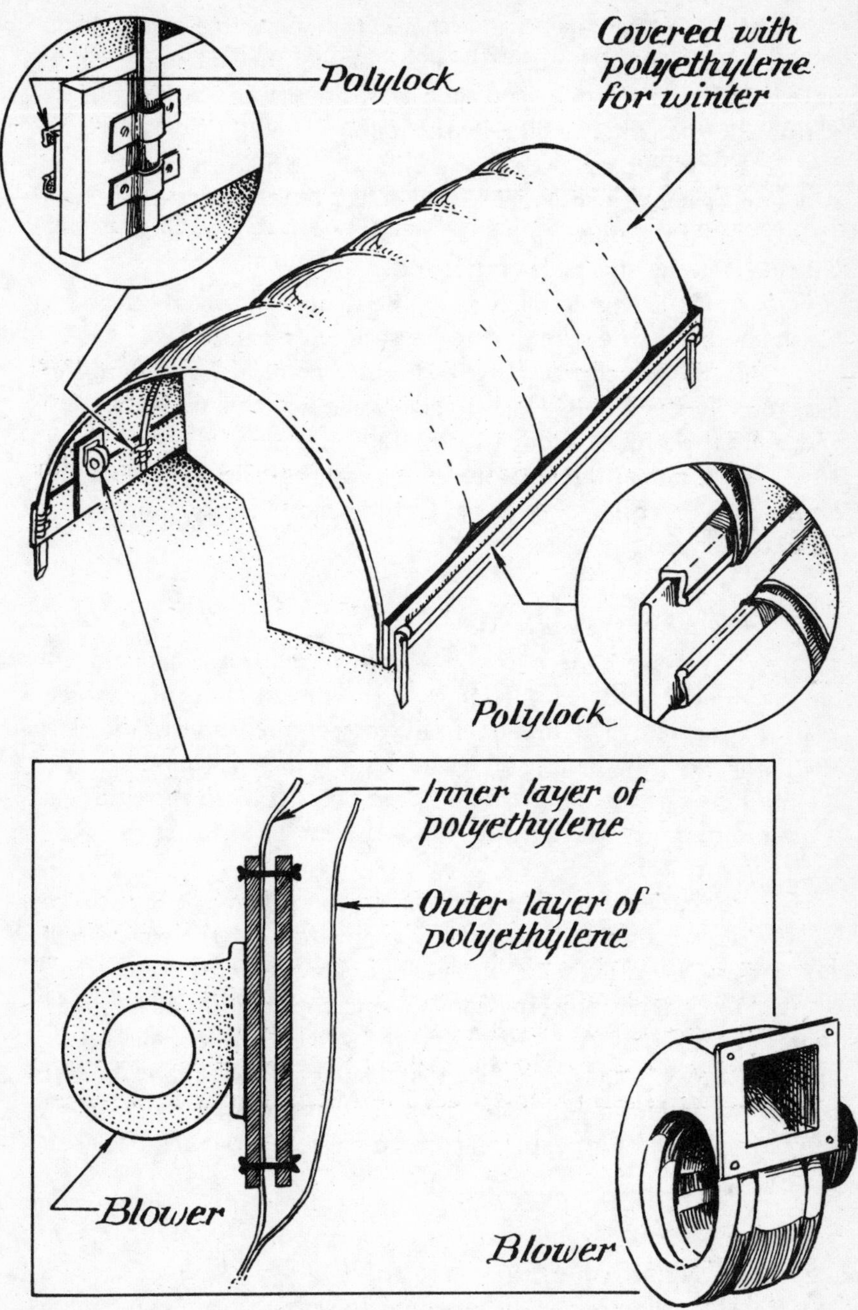

Figure 55. *Building your own inflated polyethylene crop shelter.*

4. Bend the pipe in an arch and fasten it to the second base. You now have one arch up. Walk around under the arch and see if you have enough headroom toward the edges. If you want more headroom, narrow the width and you'll raise the roof.

5. Proceed to fasten pipe arches for the full length of the structure, spacing them no more than 6 feet (2 m) apart.

6. At the ridge, fasten a 1 by 4 board the entire length of the structure, on the underside of the pipe.

7. On each side, halfway up, between the base and the ridge, fasten another 1 by 4 strip to give the structure rigidity.

8. In each corner, fasten a diagonal brace of 1 by 4 from the base to the upper frame. This will give you a structure that will withstand the force of strong winter winds.

9. On the gable ends install 2 by 10 base and wood framing fastened on the inside of the pipe. On one end the wood framing should accommodate a door.

POLYETHYLENE COVER

Now you are ready for the polyethylene cover. There are different grades of polyethylene. If you want the cover to last two or three years, buy polyethylene that has been treated to resist ultraviolet radiation; otherwise, the light will break down the material in one growing season. I use untreated polyethylene, removing it when the weather warms up, then replacing it with new material in the fall as the weather begins to turn cold.

Polyethylene is rated for thickness in mils, and for one season's use I would suggest 4 mil weight. If you plan to leave the cover on for two or three years, use 6 mil ultraviolet treated polyethylene.

You can buy polyethylene in a single sheet 14 to 40 feet (4 m to 12 m) wide. A 24-foot (7 m) roll will cover the frame with enough left over to place on the ground and cover with earth to keep the wind from blowing in under the base. Cut the polyethylene so that you have 10 feet (3 m) extra on each end to fold down and enclose the gable ends.

FASTENING POLYETHYLENE

The easiest device for fastening polyethylene is an aluminum locking strip called Polylock, which is available from the supplier where you purchase the polyethylene.

1. Fasten the Polylock to the wood base along the sides and gable ends with screws, which will hold better than nails.

2. Lay one layer of polyethylene over the frame and hold it down with rocks on the ground. Remember to leave 10 feet (3 m) at each end to cover the gable ends. Next, install the blower.

A small blower inside the grower will force air between the two layers of polyethylene. Because the air is trapped, it acts as insulation to keep the grower warm at night. You can buy a small blower from your supplier, rated at 56 cubic feet (1.6 m^3) of air per minute. The blower takes very little electricity, and you'll probably want power for lights anyway. I usually run a water line and electrical cable in one trench from house to grower.

Mount the blower on the inside of a plywood wall plate, with a hole 4 inches (10 cm) in diameter. Place the first layer of polyethylene over the outside of the wall plate and fasten it to the wall plate with a smaller piece of plywood containing a 4 inch (10 cm) hole, using bolts. Cut a 4 inch (10 cm) hole in the polyethylene.

3. Before you apply the second layer of polyethylene, tape a small piece of garden hose over the end pipe frames in each corner to allow air to reach the gable ends.

4. Spread the second layer of polyethylene over the frame and fasten both layers of polyethylene into the polylock on one side. Go to the other side, stretch both layers and fasten them into the polylock. You don't have to stretch too tightly because air inflation will take out most of the wrinkles. Do the same thing on the gable ends, folding the polyethylene as necessary.

Now you can turn on the blower and watch the polyethylene billow out into a smooth curved surface. Leave the blower on all the time and if small cuts develop in the polyethylene, use special mylar mending tape.

The Fiberglass Super Cloche

When I was in Vienna, Austria, I went to Schönbrunn Palace to see where they were growing all the bedding plants that they use at the Palace. To my surprise I discovered a fiberglass super cloche (Figure 53). I don't know where the fiberglass is manufactured in this size, but if you can find the material, it is a wonderful idea. The fiberglass sheets are 4 feet (1.2 m) wide and 32 feet (9.8 m) long, bent at the eaves, and used exactly as a large cloche. Six sections bolt together and then a 2 foot (.6 m) section is left loose so that it can be raised for ventilation. When spring comes, the units are unbolted and stacked at the end of the growing area.

This is a very simple, functional system, which you might persuade a fiberglass manufacturer to try. You could save a lot of time and effort with 5 oz (140 g) fiberglass sheets that provide the structure as well as the covering.

Adapting the Cloche to Solar Growing

The same principles apply to cloches of all sizes; get the light and heat in, absorb the heat and keep it in the grower. Traditionally, the single-glaze cloche raised the temperature around plants because the soil absorbed solar heat. Now, in addition to double glazing which we have already mentioned, let's consider other ways to absorb and hold solar heat.

In the small cloche, you can place plastic bags full of water or black tubes along the row of plants. Alternatively, a rock mulch between the rows will absorb solar energy, and I have used old bricks when they were readily available. During the day, the ends of a tunnel cloche should be left open for ventilation but should be closed at night to keep the heat inside.

In the medium-sized cloches such as frames, you can use water in 2 gallon (9 l) or even 5 gallon (23 l) black metal containers for heat storage. This might be a good place to use solar tile on the back wall, or rods if the frame is large enough. Even with double glazing you can retain more heat at night by covering the glazing with an insulating panel.

As the size of the cloche or crop shelter increases, you can use larger water containers for heat storage. I have a crop shelter 20 feet by 40 feet (6.1 by 12.2 m) in which I use a double row of 50 gallon (227 l) drums, full of water and painted black, to support a bench down the middle of the grower. You can use any of the heat storage materials we have mentioned in a large crop shelter. I used the drums because they were available, and an inexpensive way to store a large amount of heat.

When the weather warms up in the spring, you can remove the polyethylene, or other cover, and garden as you would with any outdoor plot. I would leave the heat storage materials in place year round. If you have been gardening under cloches or crop shelters, I think you'll be surprised at how much earlier your crops mature and how much bigger your yield is when you convert to solar growing.

Figure 56. A wide selection of vegetables can be grown in a solar grower.

Chapter 11

WHAT TO GROW

IN THE OUTDOOR solar garden you can grow anything you wish! The existing literature on outdoor growing is extensive, but the techniques involved in solar growing outdoors are new. (See Chapter 13.)

The number of new plant varieties is increasing each year as hybridizers improve on the older types of flowers, fruits and vegetables. If you are not already doing so, collect seed catalogs. Seed is light, easy to send by mail and it usually crosses international boundaries without any trouble. I get seed from Russia regularly. When growing plants from seed, you can honestly say that the world is your garden.

With an indoor solar garden, you can grow a wide selection of plants and defy the seasons with strawberries and cream in mid-winter. You can grow plants to make your own soap and skin lotion. You can eat better quality food and spend less on transportation. Let's take a look at some of the plants that sun energy will permit you to grow indoors.

Make a list of the food plants that best suit your family. You can save the most by growing the vegetables right from seed. In many areas, asparagus is scarce, expensive and available for a relatively short time.

If you grow asparagus from seed, you'll get 100 roots from one packet of seed! You can have it for a longer time each season and a well-constructed asparagus bed will keep producing for 100 years. In a very short time you will more than pay for your home solar grower.

Vegetables

Asparagus *(Asparagus officinalis)*. The Romans grew stalks that weighed as much as 6 ounces (170 g) each. You can grow such asparagus too. Soak seed for 48 hours at 85°F (30°C). Sow 1/2 inch (1.2 cm) deep in a planting box 3 feet (1 m) deep, with well-drained loam compost and pH7. Grow at 70°F (21°C). Seed to harvest — 3 years. 1 packet produces 100 roots. Or buy 1-year-old roots, plant 2 inches (5 cm) deep, 2 years to harvest. Don't cut, break off the stalks! Let a few stalks grow into the fern-like summer foliage which manufactures and stores food for the next season's growth energy. Plant flowers in the same bed for summer color and fragrance.

Beans

BUSH *(Phaseolus vulgaris)*. Green, wax, pole, romano, sugar pod.
LIMA *(Phaseolus limensis)*. High vitamin content.
BROAD or ENGLISH *(Vicia Faba)*.
EGYPTIAN *(Dolichos Lablab)*. From the tropics. Soak seed for 2 hours at 85°F (30°C), add a bacterial innoculant to help the roots fix nitrogen from the air, and plant 1 inch (2.5 cm) deep, 6 seeds to a pot 12 inches (30 cm) wide and 12 inches (30 cm) deep. Germinate at 75°F (24°C) and grow at 60°F (15°C).
MUNG BEAN FOR SPROUTS *(Vigna radiata)*. Soak overnight. Put 1 inch (2.5 cm) potting soil in a flat. Space seed and cover 1/4 inch (6.3 mm) deep. Cover flat with cheesecloth and keep damp at 75°F (24°C) in the dark. Harvest in 5 to 7 days, wash and serve.
SOYBEAN *(Glycine Max)*. High protein. Use as sprouts or roast like peanuts. Seed to maturity — 70 days, 50 pods per plant.

Beets *(Beta vulgaris)*. For both roots and greens try Golden Yellow and Albino White from Spain and Portugal. Soak seeds. Plant 1-1/2 inches (3.8 cm) deep in firm loam soil, pH 6.5, and grow in open sun, no shade at 60°F (16°C) days, 50°F (10°C) nights. Seed to maturity — 30 to 60 days.

Figure 57. Kitchen solar garden.

The Cole Crops

BROCCOLI *(Brassica oleracea botrytis)*. High vitamin content. Grow at cool temperature of 50°F (10°C). Seed to harvest — 55 to 90 days.

COLLARDS or BORECOLE *(Brassica oleracea acephala)*. Will stand summer heat. Excellent greens.

KALE (*Brassica* varieties). A host of varieties from Siberia, the Mediterranean, North America and China. Most like it cool. For greens.

CABBAGE *(Brassica oleracea capitata)*. Try the dwarf varieties, 4 inches (10 cm) in diameter. Seed to harvest — 60 days.

CHINESE CABBAGE (*Brassica Rapa* varieties). Very high yield, good greens, cool crop. Poultry feed, 250 grams of seed will supply foliage for 1,000 hens for 4 months. Seed germinates in 4 to 5 days at 80°F (27°C). Grow at 55°F to 65°F (13°C to

18°C) in 10 inch (25 cm) pots, 8 inch (20 cm) deep. Mix 5-10-10 fertilizer, 1 tablespoon (15 ml) per pot, and feed again in 3 to 4 weeks. Keep above 50°F (10°C).

Carrots *(Daucus Carota)*. High vitamin A content. Try the miniatures in pots 16 inches (40 cm) deep. Seed germinates in 7 to 21 days at 80°F (27°C). Grow at 50°F (10°C). Thin rows or you will get all tops. Seed to harvest — 50 to 60 days.

Corn Salad *(Valerianella* varieties). Lamb's lettuce. Salad green. Sow and grow like lettuce.

Cucumbers *(Cucumis sativus)*. Several hundred varieties. Try the English seedless, self-pollinating, bitter-free types. Float seed in water and plant those that sink. Germinate at 75°F to 80°F (24°C to 27°C). Grow at 70°F to 80°F (21°C to 27°C). Grow in tubs and support the vines on wires. Cucumbers require high heat, strong light, high humidity, heavy fertilizer, and lots of water. Liquid feed every 7 to 10 days.

Lettuce *(Lactuca sativa)*. Try the leaf varieties. Germinates in 7 days at 65°F (18°C). Grow at 60°F (15°C) days and 50°F (10°C) at night. Keep in cool partial shade. For head types, try the miniatures, one plant per pot.

Onions *(Allium Cepa)*. Try the green bunching varieties under glass (also A. *fistulosum)*. Germinate at 75°F (24°C). Grow at 55°F to 60°F (13°C to 16°C). Sow 1/2 inch (1.3 cm) deep in pots 8 inches (20 cm) deep. Seed to harvest — 60 to 70 days. Try A. *tuberosum* from China and A. *senescens* from Europe to Siberia.

Peas *(Pisum sativum)*. Try the edible pod varieties. Germinates in 21 days at 75°F (24°C). Grow at 55°F to 65°F (13°C to 18°C). Train on plastic netting. Pick young for pods, later for shelled green peas. Seed to maturity — 60 to 70 days. Cowpeas or black-eyed peas are beans *(Vigna unguiculata)*. Grow as stated for Egyptian beans.

Peppers *(Capsicum annuum)*. Sweet peppers are high in Vitamin C when eaten raw. Grown first by the Aztecs. The decorative Christmas pepper is also an edible hot pepper. Germinates in 14 days at 70°F (21°C). Grow at the same temperature. Keep night temperature above 65°F (18°C). They need lots of light and water.

Radish (*Raphanus sativus*). Four weeks from seed, you can be eating radishes. Select varieties for growing under glass. Germinate at 60°F (16°C). Grow at 50°F (10°C) or lower at night. Sow in pot 10 inches (25 cm) wide and 6 inches (15 cm) deep, so you can move to a cool location at night. Thin to 10 plants per pot. Failure to thin will result in top growth only, as will high night temperatures or not enough water. Try Chinese white for winter.

Spinach

ANNUAL (*Spinacia oleracea*). Likes 40°F to 50°F (4°C to 10°C) so it is difficult to grow inside.

PERENNIAL or NEW ZEALAND (*Tetragonia tetragoniodes*). Likes hot growing. Soak seed 24 hours. Germinates in 10 days to 3 weeks at 70°F (21°C). Grow at 70°F (21°C). The more you pick, the more it grows.

MALABAR SPINACH (*Basella alba*). A vine that may reach 30 feet (9 m) in length. Its young leaves may be cooked or used fresh in salads. A tropical plant, it likes heat.

TAMPALA (*Amaranthus tricolor*). Also a tropical plant that likes heat. Its tender young leaves are used like spinach.

Tomato (*Lycopersicon lycopersicum*). The bush type is self-topping and determinate. The vine type keeps growing to an indeterminate size. Germinate under moist conditions at 85°F (30°C). Grow at temperatures of 70°F (21°C) days, 65°F (18°C) at night. Select resistant varieties for early, mid-season or late fruiting, for greenhouse forcing. Hand-pollinate by touching each flower with a soft brush during the forenoon, every day. Feed with a high phosphate fertilizer, and keep the soil moist. Give the plants 6 hours per day of direct sunlight.

There are many other vegetables which require the space of the outdoor garden, but are best planted in the solar grower to get a head start on the season. Such food plants are cabbage, Brussels sprouts, cauliflower, corn, squash and potatoes.

Before you move young seedlings from the solar grower, harden them off in a cold frame so that they are not damaged by the cool nights of early spring.

Fruits

One of the exciting things about the home solar garden is that you can ignore geography and have delightful tropical fruits right at home. Here are some of the types you should try.

Banana *(Musa acuminata)*. Dwarf Cavendish. There is plenty of room for bananas in the two-storey solar grower. I have had 100 lbs (45 kg) of fruit from a tree grown in a box 3 feet (1 m) square, at 70°F to 75°F (21°C to 24°C).

Citrus fruits. Orange, lemon, lime, grapefruit and kumquat can all be grown at 70°F (21°C). You might like to try shaddock or pomelo as a novelty. They have fruits that may weigh 15 to 20 pounds (7 kg to 9 kg) each.

Cocona *(Solanum topiro)*. Mahogany-colored, 1 pound (500 g) fruits that are good for juice and cooking. Their taste is unique.

Bael fruit *(Aegle Marmelos)*. The fruit, which is 4 to 5 inches (10 cm to 13 cm) in diameter, makes a delicious drink.

Carambola *(Averrhoa Carambola)*. The 5 inch (13 cm) fruit may be eaten fresh or used in jams, jellies or drinks.

Fig *(Ficus carica)*. Try Brown Turkey. This tree usually produces two crops per season under glass. Other excellent varieties include the Sycamore fig *(Ficus Sycamorus)* from Africa, the peepul *(Ficus religiosa)* from India and the bush fig *(Ficus capensis)* from Africa.

Grape *(Vitis vinifera)*. There are at least 2,000 varieties. Under glass, try Black Hamburg, Muscat, Frontignan or Gros Colman. Grape vines make excellent shade for the hot summer period.

Kiwi *(Actinidia chinensis)*. A climbing vine that may reach 20 feet (6 m) with 3 inch (8 cm) tender, sweet fruits for salads or finger food. From seed, give 2 weeks at 40°F (4°C) to break dormancy. It requires a pollinator for fertilization.

Mangosteen *(Garcinia Mangostana)*. This fruit is considered by many to be the best tasting tropical fruit.

Loquat *(Eriobotrya japonica)*. Try some of the grafted varieties such as Thales, Champagne, Gold Nugget. Eat these fruits fresh or make them into jams and jellies.

You can grow dwarf varieties of any of the temperate fruits such as apples, pears, peaches, plums and apricots, but with limited space and sun heat available, these might do better outdoors. Save the solar garden for the exotic fruits that you cannot have otherwise.

Strawberries. There is something about strawberries and cream in mid-winter that makes them taste marvelous. Grow strawberries in hanging baskets, in full sun, and keep the night temperatures above 55°F (13°C). There are several improved Alpine types that you can grow from seed. Check the seed catalogs for ever-bearing or spring-bearing types that will give you fruit in winter. Runnerless types do well in pots or tubs.

Self-Care Plants

You could fill the entire solar grower with plants to improve your health, but there are some that you will want to grow along with the food and flowers.

TEAS, TONICS AND SEASONING

There are many herbs that grow too large for the solar grower and should be planted outdoors. Here are some that are less than 2 feet (60 cm) tall for the solar grower: basil, chervil, burnet, chamomile, chives, catnip, comfrey, garlic, marjoram, mint, nasturtium, oregano, parsley, rosemary, tarragon and thyme.

Go to a library and study the books on herbs. You will find that herbs have many uses; for example, chamomile makes a delicious tea and also a hair rinse for blondes. Among the herbs, you will find the ingredients to make moth repellents, oils, tonics, soaps, cosmetics, antiseptics, skin creams and lotions, spices and medicines.

Aloe barbadensis *(Aloe vera)*. There are about fifty species of *Aloe* growing around the world, many of which are used for healing the skin. The juice is widely used to treat X-ray burns to promote healing without scar tissue. I have used the juice to fade age spots on the skin. *Aloe* is an easy-to-grow succulent that you should have in your solar grower.

VITAMINS

The green plant is a very efficient chemical factory that manufactures a wide variety of products, one of which is vitamins. As long as you are growing food in your solar grower, you might as well have the benefit of plant species with high vitamin and mineral content. The following list will help you decide what to grow for vitamin content.

Stored in the body:

Vitamin A — Green and yellow vegetables, spinach, broccoli, carrots, sweet potato. Green and yellow fruits, kiwi, avocado, squash, cantaloupe.

Vitamin D — The raw materials to make vitamin D, called sterols, exist in plants. Animals and fish eat plants, and we eat fish oils, tuna and sardines to get our vitamin D. When you expose your skin to sunlight, skin oils are converted to vitamin D. With a heavy suntan, the process stops.

Vitamin E — Broccoli, Brussels sprouts, spinach, leafy greens, whole grains, wheat germ, soybeans and alfalfa.

Vitamin K — Alfalfa, safflower, soya, tomatoes, orange peel and kelp. For blood clotting.

Not stored in the body:

Vitamin B_1 — (Thiamine) Leafy greens, asparagus, beans, peas, peanuts and whole wheat yeast.

Vitamin B_2 — (Riboflavin) Leafy greens and squash.

Vitamin B_3 — (Niacin) Dates, prunes, figs, tomato juice, spinach and avocado.

Vitamin B_6 — (Pyridoxine) Cabbage, wheat bran, wheat germ, cantaloupe and brewer's yeast.

Vitamin B_5 — (Pantothenic acid) Whole grains, wheat germ, nuts, peas, green vegetables and brewer's yeast.

Vitamin B_{12} — (Cobalamin) Synthesized by intestinal bacteria in animals and not found in higher plants. We get it by eating liver, meats, eggs and dairy products.

Vitamin B_{15} — (Pangamic acid) Whole brown rice, whole grains, sesame seeds and brewer's yeast.

Vitamin C — (Ascorbic acid) Rose hips, citrus fruits, berries, leafy vegetables, tomatoes, peppers and cantaloupe.

VITAMIN GUIDELINES

Pick the produce from your solar grower in the late afternoon and you will get a higher vitamin content. During the day, the plant manufactures vitamins, while at night, it uses them in the growth process.

Eat vegetables as fresh as possible. Steam, rather than boil and save the water for soup. Don't thaw frozen vegetables before cooking.

Figure 58. Use herbs and vegetables for all-round health care.

Fragrance

Fragrance is a very pleasant, personal experience. You can enjoy even very subtle aromas in the warm humid atmosphere of the solar grower, where the conditions are favorable for producing scents. Use fragrant plants one at a time, as you do with perfume. You wouldn't wear half-a-dozen perfumes simultaneously!

Fragrance comes principally from flowers, and 60 percent of perfumed flowers are white or yellow. There are also many plants with scented leaves and these are more noticeable in the moist solar grower. The following list will help you get started exploring the vast array of fragrant plants:

BULBS

Hyacinth, crocus, narcissus, Peruvian daffodil *(Ismene calathina)* regal lily, freesia, lily of the valley, Amazon lily *(Eucharis grandiflora)*, magic lily *(Lycoris squamigera)* or tuberose *(Polianthes tuberosa)* are a few to try.

VINES

Fragrant vines include jasmine, stephanotis, honeysuckle, mignonette vine *(Anredera cordifolia)*, *Clereodendrum philippinum*, wisteria, sweet pea and Burmese honeysuckle *(Lonicera hildebrandiana)*.

NIGHT BLOOMING

For evening bloom, try evening stock *(Nicotiana)*, night phlox *(Zaluzianskya capensis)*, *Schizopetalon walkeri*, *Gladiolus tristis*, perfume plant *(Matthiola longipetala)*, and varieties of *Cestrum*.

POT CROPS

Scented geraniums (thirty varieties), heliotrope, mignonette *(Reseda odorata)*, lavender, gardenia, Persian violet *(Exacum affine)*, sweet violet, lily-of-the-valley, herbs, verbena, sweet pea, pansy, petunia, bergamot, wallflower and many other plants that may be grown in pots are fragrant.

SMALL TREES OR SHRUBS

Many varieties of small trees and shrubs are fragrant. Among others are Mexican orange *(Choisya ternata)*, mock orange *(Philadelphus)*, frangipani *(Plumeria rubra)*, eucalyptus (many varieties), ylang-ylang

(Cananaga odorata), Boronia megastigma, jessamine *(Cestrum nocturnum)*, clerodendron, oleander, *Diosma ericoides*, wintersweet *(Chimonanthus praecox)* and satinwood *(Murraya paniculata)*.

In addition to the plants just listed, there are many others you can grow to suit your needs. You may want to produce dried flowers for arrangements. Perhaps you are moving into a new home and you want to devote most of the space in the solar grower to developing landscape shrubs from cuttings. If you love to have cut flowers in the house, you can grow an assortment for year-round decoration.

Figure 59. Flowers can be practical as well as beautiful.

Chapter 12

PLANT BEAUTY CARE RECIPES

MY GRANDMOTHER kept a recipe notebook for her favorite food preparations. In the back of the notebook were a few of the recipes that she used for her own beauty care. Long before there were drugstores, people all over the world used plant derivatives to provide for their well-being. Many of the things they used can still be grown at home, either in your solar grower or outdoors in the yard.

The advantage of preparing your own beauty care products are similar to those mentioned for growing your own food.

1. Additives. You can use only those materials which you know are beneficial for your body. You do not have to gamble on unknown chemical additives.

2. Chemical residues. You can avoid contaminated plants grown using unknown chemicals to control pests, disease and weeds.

3. Freshness. Most plants begin to lose the ingredients valuable for beauty care soon after they are harvested. Dried materials are a poor substitute for the freshness of your own home-grown plants.

4. Variety. You have a wider choice of natural compounds, many of which may not be readily available in the drugstore. Even in the newer health food shops you can't always find a wide selection of natural herb products or if you do, they are dried.

I am not suggesting that you ignore everything new in beauty care, but that you be selective and rediscover a lot of the good things from the past that we have perhaps forgotten.

The following recipes (with one exception) are limited to plant material that you can grow at home. If you live close to a company that sells botanicals (preparations made from plants) you can widen your scope and try plant extracts from all over the world.

Before you apply a large quantity of any homemade preparation to your skin, be sure to test for irritation. Dab a little on the inside of your arm and leave it overnight. If the skin turns red, do not use the product.

Preparations For Your Hair

Human hair is naturally acid and washing with alkaline soaps or shampoos can upset the acid balance and damage your hair. The soapwort shampoo is slightly acid.

SOAPWORT SHAMPOO

1/2 cup (125 ml) soapwort juice
2 cups (500 ml) chamomile water (for blondes)
2 cups (500 ml) rosemary water (for brunettes)

To make soapwort juice, put 1 or 2 branches in a vegetable juicer and extract the juice. Rinse the juicer with a tablespoon (15 ml) of cider vinegar in a pint (500 ml) of water. To make chamomile or rosemary water, put 3 teaspoons (15 ml) of fresh leaves in a cooking pot that is not made of aluminum. Pour 1 pint (500 ml) boiling water over the leaves. Cover the pot tightly and let steep for two hours. Strain the cooled solution through cheesecloth. Store in the refrigerator.

Add the 2 cups (500 ml) of herb water to the soapwort juice and stir gently. Use as you would any shampoo. If you need more suds, add more soapwort juice.

Soapwort is *Saponaria officinalis*, sometimes called bouncing bet. The plant is easy to grow and reaches a height of 3 feet (1 m). You can buy seed or plants at the same nurseries that carry the well-known herbs chamomile and rosemary.

Do not eat the leaves or seeds of soapwort, which may contain toxic substances.

YUCCA SHAMPOO

4 ounces (125 ml) of yucca root decoction
2 cups (500 ml) rosemary water

To make the yucca decoction, chop up 4 ounces (125 ml) of yucca root. Put into one pint (500 ml) of boiling water, and cover at once. Boil for fifteen minutes, turn off the heat and let steep for thirty minutes. Strain and cool. Store in the refrigerator. When chilled, add rosemary water and perhaps a drop of your favorite perfume.

Soapweed, *Yucca glauca*, grows to nearly 3 feet (1 m) tall and is as wide as it is tall. It is probably best planted outdoors in full sun. Check your nursery catalog for a source.

LEMON AND ROSEMARY HAIR SET

2 lemons
2 teaspoons (10 ml) rosemary leaves
1 whole egg, beaten

Chop the lemons into small pieces and boil in 1 pint (500 ml) of water. When the water is boiling, add 2 teaspoons (10 ml) of rosemary leaves and the beaten egg. Cover the pot. Turn off the heat and let steep for fifteen minutes. Strain through cheesecloth or gauze and refrigerate. This hair set takes a long time to dry but it holds well, even on a damp, rainy day.

The best lemon to grow at home in your solar grower is Citrus Lemon variety Meyer, commonly called Meyer lemon. The fruit is about 3 inches (8 cm) in diameter with a thick skin. The plant will grow well in cool temperatures as low as 50°F (10°C).

QUINCE SEED HAIR SET

1 tablespoon (15 ml) quince seed
1 tablespoon (15 ml) eau de cologne

Add 1 tablespoon (15 ml) of quince seed to 1 pint (500 ml) of boiling water. Turn off the heat and simmer until the mixture thickens. Add 1 tablespoon (15 ml) of your favorite eau de cologne and stir. Store in the refrigerator.

Quince, *Chaenomales speciosa*, is an attractive shrub for the yard. It grows about 6 feet (2 m) high and has rose-colored flowers. Make sure that you buy a variety that produces fruit.

FLAXSEED HAIR SET

1 tablespoon (15 ml) flaxseed
1 tablespoon (15 ml) chamomile leaves
1 whole egg

Add a tablespoon (15 ml) of flaxseed to 1/4 cup (60 ml) of boiling water and simmer until the mixture thickens. Place this in the blender with the raw whole egg and mix until it is smooth. Put 1 tablespoon (15 ml) of chamomile leaves in 1 pint (500 ml) of water, bring to a boil and let steep for ten minutes. Add the flax and egg to the chamomile water and simmer for five minutes. Strain and store in the refrigerator.

Flax, *Linum usitatissimum*, is an annual that grows to 3 feet (1 m) high with blue or white flowers. This is the commercial flax, not the garden plant with yellow summer bloom. You can grow the plants in your solar grower or out in the yard.

SCENTED VINEGAR HAIR RINSE

1 quart (1 l) cider vinegar
6 tablespoons (80 ml) of fresh flower petals; violet, lavender, rose, honeysuckle, marigold or your choice
1 ounce (28 g) rosemary water
1 ounce (28 g) mint water
1 ounce (28 g) thyme water

To make the herb waters, put 3 teaspoons (15 ml) of fresh leaves in a cooking pot that is not made of aluminum. Pour 1 pint (500 ml) of boiling water over the leaves. Cover the pot and let steep for two hours. Strain and refrigerate.

Put the fresh flowers, one kind only, in the quart (1 l) of vinegar and let steep for two weeks. Shake daily, strain and rebottle. Add the herb water to the vinegar. Use 1 cup (250 ml) of the mixture per quart (1 l) of water.

You'll find the herbs and flowers easy to produce in your solar grower, and if you have apple trees, you can make your own cider vinegar. Some of the marigolds are very strong-scented, and you may want to use less than 6 tablespoons (80 ml) of petals. You can use petals of any scented flowers that you like.

Recipes for Your Face

My grandmother never used soap on her face. Instead she used herb steaming occasionally and elder cleaner often.

HERB STEAMING

Put 1 cup (250 ml) of fresh elder flowers into a pot of boiling water, turn off the heat and let steep for five minutes. Reheat. Use a towel for a cloth tent over your head and expose your face to the steam for five minutes. Close the pores with an astringent such as witch hazel or chilled chamomile water.

Elder is *Sambucus canadensis* in North America and *Sambucus nigra* in Europe. The plant grows to about 8 feet (2.4 m) tall, has white flowers and black berries. The two species mentioned above make attractive shrubs for the yard and the berries will give you tasty jams or wine. The red-berried species are poisonous.

ELDER WATER FACE CLEANSER

1 cup (250 ml) buttermilk
2 tablespoons (30 ml) honey
5 tablespoons (75 ml) fresh elder blossoms

Heat the buttermilk and soak the elder flowers in it, simmering for one hour. Turn off the heat and steep for three hours. Reheat. Strain and add the honey. Keep under refrigeration. Apply liberally to the face and rinse with chamomile water.

NATURAL SOAP

The original, natural bar of soap is the bulb of a lily, *Chlorogalum pomeridianum*, known as amole or soap plant. The bulb has a fibrous outer husk like the coconut. Take off the husk and you'll find a natural bar of soap about 2 inches (5 cm) wide and 4 inches (10 cm) long. This soap is non-alkaline and can be used as you would any bar soap.

You can grow amole in your solar grower. The plant reaches 3 to 4 feet (90 cm to 120 cm) and has white flowers streaked with purple which open in the afternoon. Available from specialty seed companies in western North America.

MAKE YOUR OWN SOAP

2 pounds (900 g) pure beef tallow, rendered
2 pounds (900 g) sal soda (sodium carbonate decahydrate)
1 pound (450 g) salt
1 ounce (28 g) gum camphor
1 ounce (28 g) oil of bergamot
1 ounce (28 g) borax

Put all the ingredients in a large pot, boil slowly for an hour and stir often. Let stand until cool, then warm the mixture again until it pours. Pour into molds of your choice. After eight hours, dip the molds in cold water and remove the bars from the molds. Cure with good air circulation around each bar for eight weeks. At the end of eight weeks, touch a bit of soap to your tongue. If it stings, cure the bars for a longer time.

This is obviously not soap from plants grown at home but you might like to try an old soap recipe. The sal soda (sodium carbonate decahydrate) is less caustic then lye (sodium or potassium hydroxide).

CUCUMBER COLD CREAM

1/2 ounce (14 g) white wax
2 ounces (56 g) almond oil
2 ounces (56 g) fresh cucumber juice

Put the wax and almond oil in a small pan and melt. Add the cucumber juice very slowly, beating the solution with a fork until all the juice is incorporated. Pour into a jar and let cool. Use for a face cleanser and rinse with chamomile water.

Flower Oils

For fragrance to use in face and bath preparations, you can make your own oils from flower petals in at least two ways.

Enfleurage is the process of exposing odorless fats or oils to fresh flower petals. The oils absorb the fragrance of the petals and you have flower oil.

ROSE OIL

1 pound (450 g) red rose buds
4 quarts (4 l) olive oil

Beat the rose buds to a fine pulp in a mortar. Put the petals in an earthen pot and add the olive oil. Let the pot sit in the sun for one month, stirring occasionally. When the oil smells like roses, the enfleurage process is complete. Heat the oil until warm, press and strain through gauze. Pour into a labelled, dark glass jar and refrigerate.

GARDENIA OIL

1/2 pound (250 g) gardenia petals
1 pint (500 ml) olive oil

Place a piece of olive oil-soaked cotton in the bottom of an enamel pan. Spread out fresh gardenia petals on the cotton. Cover with olive oil-soaked cloth. Alternate these layers until all the petals are used. Cover the pan with a sheet of glass. Change the petals and replace with fresh cloth every twenty-four hours, until the oil takes up the fragrance. Squeeze the perfumed oil out of the cotton into a dark brown bottle. Keep in the refrigerator or a cool closet.

The second method of making flower oil is by extraction.

1/2 to 1 pound (225 g to 450 g) of your favorite fragrant petals such as violet, jasmine, honeysuckle, etc.

Place a thin layer of petals in the bottom of a shallow enamel pan. Cover the petals with 1 inch (2.5 cm) of natural soft water. Set the pan in the sun for three or four days. When you see a film or droplets of oil floating on the surface, collect them by soaking into a cotton swab. Squeeze the swab out into a dark bottle. Leave the bottle open to the air until the water evaporates. Close the bottle and refrigerate. Repeat as needed.

This is a slow process but the rewards are great. You would have to pay several hundred dollars per ounce (28 ml) for flower oils purchased from a botanical supply company.

Herbal Baths

1 handful fresh balm leaves
1 handful almond-scented geranium leaves
1 handful plantain leaves

Put all the leaves into 1 quart (1 l) of boiling water and steep for fifteen or twenty minutes. Strain and put 8 tablespoons (125 ml) into your bath water.

Balm, *Mellisa officinalis*, is a member of the mint family with lemon-scented leaves, which grows about 2 feet (60 cm) high. Grown in your solar grower, this plant will give the air a pleasant lemon fragrance.

Plantain, *Plantago major*, is a common dooryard weed that can be grown from seed in your solar grower. The leaves form a rosette, close to the ground and the flower stalks are about a foot (30 cm) high.

If you use dried herbs, you can sew a handful into small gauze bags with a drawstring, and use them like large tea bags dipped into the bath water.

VINEGAR AND HERB BATH

2 ounces (56 g) fresh thyme, spearmint, rosemary, lavender and sage, or 1 ounce (28 g) each of dried leaves
1/2 ounce (14 g) of psyllium (the juice squeezed from the plantain seed)
1 ounce (28 g) of expressed cranberry
4 teaspoons (5 ml) 75 percent alcohol

Bruise the herbs thoroughly by crushing them and place them in a stone jar. Add a quart (1 l) of boiling vinegar and cover tightly. Steep for two weeks, shaking now and then with the cover on. Strain off the vinegar.

In a separate bottle mix the psyllium, cranberry and alcohol until the ingredients are dissolved. Add this mixture to the vinegar and let stand for three days. Filter this liquid through linen and pour into a bottle with a tight cap. Add 4 to 6 tablespoons (60 ml to 80 ml) to your bath water.

Psyllium is the expressed juice of plantain seed, or the juice squeezed from the seed. For cranberry, use the juice squeezed from fresh, whole berries.

You can add fragrance to any bath by using a few drops of your favorite flower oil in the bath water.

Bath Salts

2 cups (500 ml) of borax
40 drops of flower oil

Place the borax in a wide-mouthed jar and add 20 drops of flower oil. Blend with a wooden spoon and cover. Let the mixture sit overnight and add 20 more drops of flower oil. Cover tightly and let sit for another day. Add 2 or 3 tablespoons (30 ml to 45 ml) to your bath water.

Potpourris

A potpourri is a mixture of dried flowers, leaves, oils and spices which is usually kept in an open jar to perfume the air in a room.

A sachet is a little bag containing a potpourri for use in bureau drawers or closets to perfume clothing and linens.

There are literally hundreds of flower and leaf scents from plants that you can grow at home and use for potpourris. From the many that you might grow, here is a basic list of the reliable varieties to help you get started.

Flowers and leaves: mint, rose, thyme, geranium, rosemary, verbena, lavender.

Spices: clove, cinnamon, nutmeg, lemon and orange peel.

Fixatives: orris, vetiver.

Orris is the dried, powdered root of *Iris germanica* or *Iris pallida*. The plant grows about 2 feet (60 cm) tall and will survive outdoors at temperatures down to 10°F (-12°C). If you live in a colder climate, I would suggest planting it in your solar grower. Some people have a sensitivity to orris. Use with caution.

Vetiver is the dried, powdered root of *Vetiveria zizanioides*, or Khus Khus, a tropical grass plant. The plant grows about 6 feet (2 m) tall and makes an attractive accent for a sunny corner of the solar grower. For good growth keep the temperature at 55°F (13°C), or higher.

COLLECTING AND STORING HERBS

1. Collect the plants before 10 a.m. for the highest perfume content.

2. Harvest more than you think you'll need because the herbs shrink when they are dried.

3. To dry whole plants, hang them in a cool, dry, airy place for two weeks.

4. To dry leaves and petals, spread them out on cheesecloth in a dry location out of the sun.

5. If you are in a hurry, or if the weather is bad, place leaves or petals in the oven. Leave the door open and set at the lowest temperature. Turn frequently.

6. For citrus peelings, scrape off the inner white surface and dry in the air or the oven.

7. Avoid plants that have been sprayed with any kind of chemicals.

8. Store herbs in a cool, dry, dark place, in containers with airtight covers.

GENERAL PROCEDURE AND MATERIALS FOR STOCK

1 quart (1 l) of major scent dried ingredients
1 pint (500 ml) of minor scent materials
1 ounce (28 g) powdered spice or peeling
20 drops of flower oil
16 ounces (450 g) of orris or vetiver

Mix the dried ingredients in a bowl lined with wax paper. In a separate bowl mix the spices and peelings. Cut the peelings into little pieces about ⅛ inch (3.2 mm) square. Mix in the spices and peel. Now add the flower oils and let the bowl sit for two hours, sealed with wax paper. Add the fixative of orris or vetiver and mix thoroughly again. Place the mixture in an earthen pot with a tight cover, and let it cure for three days in a dark, cool location. Open the crock and put the potpourri into appropriate sachets or jars.

Using the above materials and procedures, you can make the following recipes or some of your own invention.

GRANDMOTHER'S FAVOURITE SACHET

2 ounces (56 g) rosemary
2 ounces (56 g) spearmint
2 ounces (56 g) rose petal
1 ounce (28 g) orris
2 ounces (56 g) orange peel

POTPOURRI D'AVIGNON

4 ounces (125 g) rose petal
4 ounces (125 g) lavender
2 ounces (56 g) rose leaf
1 ounce (28 g) orris
¼ ounce (7 g) clove
¼ ounce (7 g) cinnamon
¼ ounce (7 g) orange peel
¼ ounce (7 g) rose oil

SPRING BOUQUET
4 ounces (125 g) violet petal
1 ounce (28 g) rose petal
2 drops bitter almond oil
1 ounce (28 g) lime peel
2 ounces (56 g) orris
1 ounce (28 g) fruit tree petal

SUMMER SWEETNESS
8 ounces (250 g) lilac petal
4 ounces (125 g) rose leaf
2 ounces (56 g) thyme
2 ounces (56 g) spearmint
1 ounce (28 g) rosemary
1 ounce (28 g) scented geranium leaf
4 ounces (28 g) orris

DREAM PILLOW SACHET
8 ounces (250 g) balsam fir tips
2 ounce (56 g) thyme
1 ounce (28 g) lime peel
1 ounce (28 g) rosemary
2 ounces (56 g) orris

When you are making a potpourri, keep a notebook handy and write down the amount of each ingredient that you use. Otherwise, you may create a masterpiece and forget what you put in it.

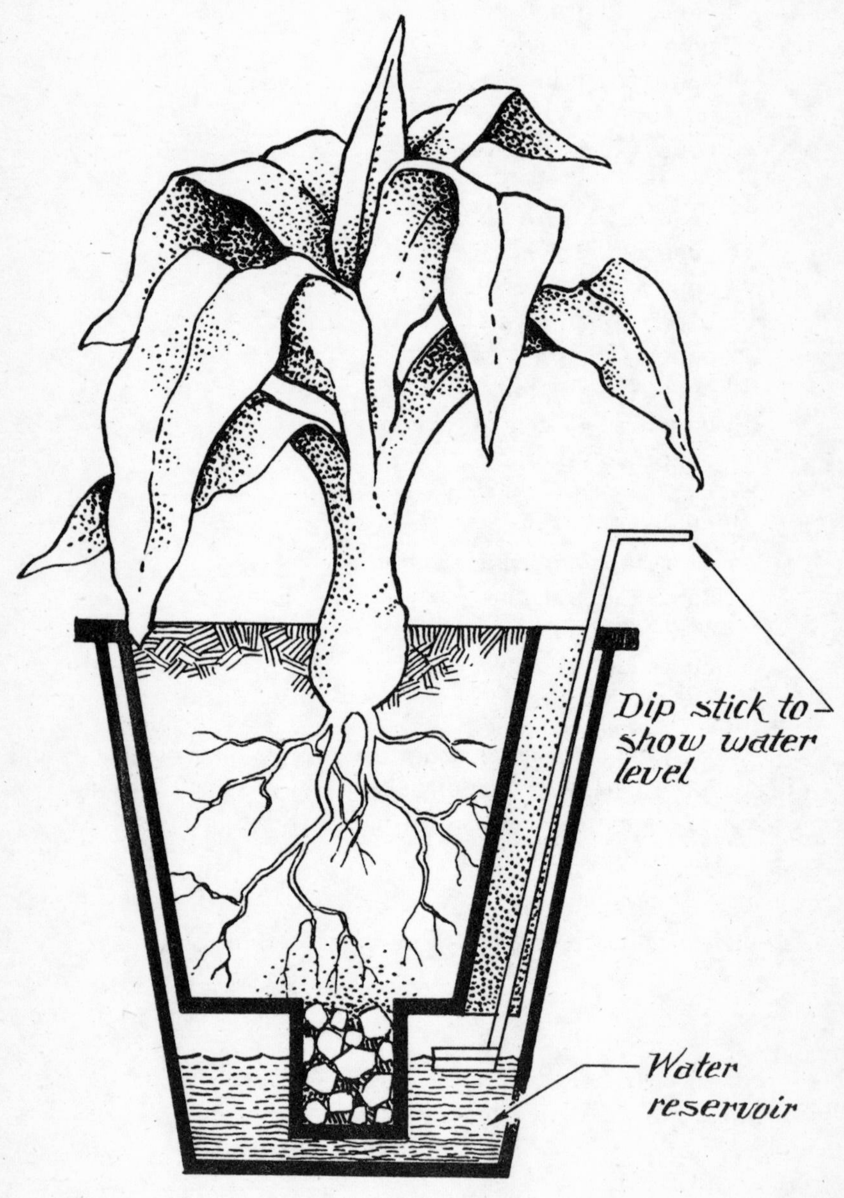

Figure 60. Self-watering pot.

Chapter 13

SOLAR GROWING TECHNIQUES

WHEN YOU BRING plants from all over the world into your solar grower, you want to reproduce their natural habitat conditions as closely as possible. In the library, you will find an encyclopedia of horticulture which will tell you where your plant comes from. This is your best clue to the proper conditions needed by your plant for solar growing.

Wherever the plant is native, the particular climate involves light, heat, water, carbon dioxide, fertilizer and soil.

Light

If your plant is a ground cover, growing in the shade of larger shrubs and trees, the light intensity it needs may be only 50 foot-candles. If the plant is an alpine bluebell growing in full sunlight, then it is used to 10,000 foot-candles. If you hold a lighted candle one foot (30 cm) away from a one foot square (.09 m^2) of white paper, then the paper receives one foot-candle. You can measure the foot-candles in your solar grower with a camera that has a built-in light meter, as follows:

1. Lay a piece of white paper where you intend to grow the plant.
2. Set the film speed indicator at 100 and the shutter aperture at f4.
3. Now read the shutter speed, which will give you the approximate light intensity in foot-candles.

Under a regular 100-watt bulb this procedure should give you about 125 foot-candles.

In addition to the intensity of the light, you must consider the duration of the light in the native habitat of your plant. Plants such as azalea, gloxinia and African violet require a long day and a short night in order to produce flowers. Others, such as gardenia, poinsettia and Christmas cactus, need a short day and a long night for flowering. When you purchase plants, ask whether they are long- or short-day plants and locate them accordingly in the solar grower.

With too little light, leaf tips may discolor, leaves and buds drop, and the plant will lose vigor. With the wrong day length, some plants will not produce flowers. In your solar garden, try to duplicate the light conditions of the native habitat.

Heat

The same guidelines apply to heat as mentioned above for light. Seed from the mild sub-tropical climates will germinate readily. Seed from cold climate alpine plants require a chilling period, such as occurs in the native location, in order to trigger germination. Likewise, seed from the hot tropics need warm treatment in order to germinate. The same is true of the growing plant. You get healthy, vigorous plants when the temperatures in your solar grower are close to those of the native environment.

Water

Consider the way in which plants are watered in the natural setting. The rain and snow fall, then the ground absorbs the water so that there is a constant supply to the roots of the plants. You can't supply rainfall in the solar garden but you can provide a constant source of moisture from the bottom, with self-watering pots or capillary mats (Figure 60). This type of watering is suitable for the plants that come from areas of heavy rainfall, where the soil is often saturated.

Obviously, plants from the desert need little water because they are adapted to reduce water loss from the leaves or stem.

In between rain forest and desert plants are most of the plants which are easy to water with a spaghetti tube system (Figure 38). The roots of plants need oxygen as well as water, and using the spaghetti tube system with a time clock lets you alternate water and air penetration of the growing medium.

When the sun is out and temperatures are up, then plants are using water. When it is cloudy or dull and the temperature is down, then plants are not using water. Young, actively growing plants need more water than mature plants.

One of the best moisture meters is an educated finger. As you become familiar with the conditions in your solar garden, you will get so that you can stick a finger into the soil and know whether the plant needs water or not.

Fertilizer

When you buy fertilizer, look for the three-number formula on the bag or bottle. This number, such as 5-10-5, stands for the percentage of nitrogen, phosphate and potash. In general, as has already been mentioned, nitrogen N, goes into foliage growth; phosphate P, goes to production of flower and fruit; potash K, goes into stem sturdiness and root growth. Also, look for the minor, or trace elements on the package. Trace elements are necessary for growth, even though the amounts are very small. If you use a fish emulsion or seaweed fertilizer, you will get all the trace elements.

Plants are really like people in that they like to eat often. If you halve the dilution of fertilizer given on the package and feed every time you water, your plants will respond with good growth and fabulous flowers.

Carbon Dioxide

Perhaps the most overlooked plant nutrient is carbon dioxide. Carbon makes up about 45 percent of a plant by dry weight and the only source of the carbon is the carbon dioxide in the atmosphere. The normal carbon dioxide content of the air is 300 parts per million.

When you go into your solar grower in the morning, the carbon dioxide content may be up to 400 or 450 parts per million, because the plants have been giving off carbon dioxide during the night. About six hours after sunrise, the carbon dioxide content is down to about 150 parts per million, because the plants use the carbon dioxide to manufacture starch, carbohydrates and sugars. Commercial growers use carbon dioxide generators to raise the level to 1,000 to 1,500 parts per million, for three reasons.

1. To increase the yield. In crops such as tomatoes and lettuce, the yield increases by 50 percent with the higher levels of carbon dioxide. This is because there is more carbon available for the growth of tissues.

2. To improve the quality. Carbon is one of the key elements in the sugars which give many vegetables their flavor, and flowers their color and size.

3. To provide early maturity. If there is plenty of carbon available, then growth proceeds more rapidly and flowers and fruits mature sooner than when lack of carbon acts as a limiting factor to growth.

There are several ways to raise the carbon dioxide level in your solar grower.

1. When the carbon dioxide is down to 150 parts per million, around noon, open the door or ventilators and let the outside air in to bring the carbon dioxide concentration back up to 300 parts per million.

2. Keep the air circulating with a small ceiling fan. If you have a door or window into the house, open it. Inside the house people are exhaling carbon dioxide, and cooking often produces carbon dioxide as a by-product. You can add some carbon dioxide by talking to your plants! I have a friend who keeps rabbit hutches under the benches to provide additional carbon dioxide.

3. Use organic mulches which release carbon dioxide as a by-product of decomposition. This suggests that you might have a compost bin inside your solar grower. The difficulty with the organic mulches is that they release nearly all their carbon dioxide in about four weeks and should be replaced.

Compost

There are several very neat boxes available for composting under the benches in your solar grower. Put a layer of plant refuse 3 or 4 inches (7.5 cm to 10 cm) thick in the bottom of the box. Add a light dressing of ammonium sulphate and 1 inch (2.5 cm) of soil. Arrange a 6 inch (15 cm) layer of plant debris covered with lime, then another 6 inch (15 cm) layer covered with ammonium sulphate and soil. Keep the lime and ammonium sulphate separate. Repeat until the box is full, then dress the top with soil, poke some holes into the center and water thoroughly. Water again in a month, if the compost dries out. You really don't need to turn the pile. In two or three months you'll have rich loamy compost, plus the benefits of the carbon dioxide released.

Soils

Here again for guidelines to good solar growing, go back to the native soils in which the plant grows. For the deep beds, where you grow the root crops, use a loose, friable sandy loam garden soil and one-third garden compost. If you live where soils are not readily available, you have several choices:

1. Purchase ready-made potting mixes.
2. Mix your own with peat moss, vermiculite, perlite or composted sawdust.
3. Grow hydroponically, using water and an inert aggregate such as shale.
4. Find a commercial grower of greenhouse crop plants and see what he is using for a growing medium. He might very well sell you some. A good all-purpose mix is two parts garden soil, one part compost or leaf mold and one part clean sand.

If you have trouble with a particular soil mix, send a sample to the nearest government agency for a soil test.

The fact that you can grow many plants hydroponically, without soil, indicates that one function of soil is to support the plant mechanically. Another function is to provide a place where the microorganisms can break down old leaves and plants to form organic fertilizers. As long as you provide the fertilizer food for your plants you can use soilless mixes successfully.

If you are growing legumes, such as peas and beans, in a soilless mix then add a bacterial innoculant which helps the roots fix nitrogen from the air. You can get the innoculant where seed is sold and get much better growth from your peas and beans.

Seed Germination

To germinate seed successfully you need the following: adequate moisture, good air circulation, soil temperature of 70°F (21°C), correct light conditions, proper sowing depth and pre-chilling treatment. This information is on the back of most packets of seed or in seed catalogs.

One of the easiest ways to get the 70°F (21°C) bottom heat is to use a small tray with an electric cable that has a built-in thermostat set for the correct temperature. You'll find these trays in most garden shops.

Cuttings

You can use the same bottom heat tray to root cuttings. Because the cutting has no root system to supply water, you need to keep the air around the top of the cuttings moist all the time. Put a plastic tent over the tray so that water condenses inside and keeps the humidity high.

Whenever you take a cutting, be sure to slice through a node. Dip the cutting in a rooting powder and place in the soil. If the cutting is hard and woody, bruise or scar a portion near the base.

Keep your rooting tray in bright light so there will be sun energy available to produce roots.

Pest and Disease Control

You can control pests and disease in your solar garden without using toxic chemicals. Here are some guidelines:

1. Throw away, or burn, badly diseased or infested plants. Doing this is much better than spreading the problem through the rest of the solar garden. If you have a choice plant, and chemical control is the only way to save it, take the plant out of the house to apply the chemical.

2. Keep the solar garden clean. Pick off dead flowers and leaves and put them in the compost.

3. For control of the adult forms of aphis, whitefly, mealy bug and mites, try one of the following:

- Put one tablespoon (15 ml) of liquid detergent in a gallon (4.5 l) of water. Douse the plant thoroughly and let it sit for two hours. Then rinse the plant under the faucet.

- Purchase one of the liquid plastic products made to prevent wilting such as Wilt-pruf, Foliagard or Poly-grabber. Apply this to the plant thoroughly. The substance will not harm the plant but will gum up the mouth parts of the insects so they cannot chew leaves or suck juices.
- There are various products made from diatomaceous earth that you sprinkle dry on the insects which then become dehydrated. Diatomaceous earth is the chalk-like skeletal remains of certain types of algae. Be sure that you don't use diatomaceous earth on the vegetables you plan to eat, because these products are toxic.
- Place 3 tablespoons (45 ml) of spirits of ammonia in a saucer and put it close to the plant. Cover the whole plant plus the saucer with a plastic tent and leave it overnight. The ammonia will turn to vapor and kill many of the insects. You may also kill the plant, so put one leaf under a small tent as a trial. If the leaf is damaged, don't use ammonia with the whole plant.
- If you have good air circulation, plant diseases never get started. This is most necessary during the winter months.

You can have a lot of fun as you begin to think solar. If you join a plant society, you can share solar techniques with your fellow gardeners. You learn by experimenting! The term "green thumb" was originally applied to the English stove house grower who handled algae-covered pots all day and came home with a green thumb. It's this simple. The more you grow, the more you know!

Resource List

ONCE YOU HAVE decided to have a home solar grower greenhouse and heat trap, you need to know where to get up-to-date information, as well as where to get the necessary supplies. The following lists are by no means complete but will help you get started.

YELLOW PAGES

There are so many new companies marketing lean-to greenhouses and solar and greenhouse supplies that the best way to locate them is in the yellow pages of your local telephone book, listed under greenhouses, gardening, seed companies, and solar.

SEED COMPANIES

More and more seed companies are listing gardening and greenhouse supplies in their catalogues.

RETAIL STORES

Many garden centers and nurseries carry the supplies that you may need, and some have well-informed sales clerks.

CANADIAN SOURCES

*Please note that toll-free numbers work only within Canada.

Home Greenhouse Supplies

Applied Hydroponics of Canada, 2215 Walkley, Montreal, Quebec H4B 2J9. Tel.: 514-489-3803; Fax: 514-489-3805. Check this out for the equipment and supplies you need in order to have fresh salads all winter.

Equipment Consultants and Sales, 2241 Dunwin Drive, Mississauga, Ontario L5L 1A3. Tel.: 416-828-5925; Fax: 416-820-0630. Carries the English Humex line of greenhouse equipment and Stewart planters and pots.

Gardenponics, 186 Joicey Blvd., Toronto, Ontario M5M 2V2. Tel.: 416-482-3343. Complete automated hydroponic systems and supplies.

Stokes Seeds Ltd., Box 10, 39 James St., St. Catharines, Ontario L2R 6R6. Tel.: 416-688-4300; Fax: 416-684-8411. Stokes Seeds now has a general store section in their catalogue with all kinds of garden and greenhouse items, as well as a retail store section.

Solar Products

Canadian Solar Industries Association, 67A Sparks St., Ottawa, Ontario K1P 5A5. Tel.: 613-736-9077; Fax: 613-736-8938. Solar reports, list of manufacturers.

Energy Alternatives, 7 Morewater Road, Lasqueti Island, British Columbia V0R 2J0. Tel.: 604-333-8898.

Nu-Tec Engineering Ltd., 3104 S.E. Marine Drive, Vancouver, British Columbia V5F 2H4. Tel.: 604-435-6963.

Photovoltaic Systems: A Buyer's Guide, Energy Mines and Resources Canada, 580 Booth St., Ottawa, Ontario K1A 0E4.

Prometheus Energy Systems, 400 Creditstone, Suite 33, Concord, Ontario L4K 3Z3. Tel./Fax: 416-660-7868. Complete photovoltaic systems and direct current appliances.

Reonac Energy Systems, 1475 Begin St., Montreal, Quebec H4R 1V8. Tel.: 514-331-5871.

Solar Innovations Inc., 7126 Barlow Trail S.E., Calgary, Alberta T2C 2E1. Tel.: 403-279-6222; Fax: 403-279-6765.

Soltek Solar Energy Ltd., 2-745 Vanalman Avenue, Victoria, British Columbia V8Z 3B6. Tel.: 604-727-7720; Fax: 604-727-2135. Gives product lists and supplies complete photovoltaic systems.

Sunset Solar Systems Ltd., Box 1327, Assiniboia, Saskatchewan S0H 0B0. Tel.: 306-642-4240; Fax: 306-642-4420.

Thermomax, 6702 Rajpur Place, Victoria, British Columbia V8X 3X1. Tel.: 604-652-6002, 800-776-5277. Vacuum tube solar hot water system providing year-round performance.

Information

SOLAR

Brace Research Institute, P.O. Box 900, MacDonald College, McGill University, St. Anne de Bellevue, Quebec H9X 1C0. Tel.: 514-398-7833. Books and plans for small greenhouses and solar devices.

Solar Energy Society of Canada, 15 York St., Suite 3, Ottawa, Ontario K1N 5S7. Tel.: 613-236-4594. Publishes *SOL* magazine. Joining this society will give you access to a wealth of information on all aspects of solar technology.

Solar Thermal Research Laboratory, University of Waterloo, Waterloo, Ontario N2L 3G1. Tel.: 519-885-1211, ext. 6844. The university operates a laboratory on glazing.

PLANTS AND GROWING

Your nearest botanical garden or arboretum has gardens and greenhouses where you can see all kinds of plants and get information on their culture.

Canadian Gardening, Camar Publications Ltd., 130 Spy Court, Markham, Ontario L3R 5H6. Tel.: 416-475-8440.

Earthkeeper Magazine, 99 Edinburgh Road South, Guelph, Ontario N1H 5P5. Tel.: 519-763-9357; Fax: 519-836-0324. Environmental magazine—March-April 1991 was a special solar issue with resource lists.

A *Fleur de Pot*, HortiCom Inc., 1449 William St., Sillery, Quebec G1S 4G5. Newsletter on indoor plants. Also *House Plant Forum* in English.

Gardens-West, Cornwall Publishing Co., Box 2680, Vancouver, British Columbia. Tel.: 604-732-4411; Fax: 604-732-4423.

Harrowsmith, Camden House Publishing, 7 Queen Victoria Road,

Camden East, Ontario K0K 1J0. Tel.: 613-378-6661. Covers country living and gardening.

The Island Grower, Greenheart Publications, R.R. #4, Sooke, British Columbia V0S 1N0.

TLC for plants, Gardenvale Publishing Co., 1 Pacifique, St. Anne de Bellevue, Quebec H9X 1C5.

The Twenty-First Century Gardener, Growers Press, Inc., P.O. Box 189, Princeton, British Columbia V0X 1W0. Tel.: 604-295-7755. For greenhouse and hydroponic growers.

UNITED STATES SOURCES

*Please note that toll-free numbers work only within the United States.

Home Greenhouse Supplies

Applied Hydroponics, 3135 Kerner Boulevard, San Rafael, California 94901. Tel.: 800-634-9999. Equipment and supplies.

Charley's Greenhouse Supplies, 1569 Memorial Highway, Mt. Vernon, Washington 98273. Tel.: 800-322-4707, 206-428-2626. Greenhouse supplies for the home greenhouse.

East Coast Hydroponics, 432 Castleton Avenue, Staten Island, N.Y. 10301. Tel.: 718-727-9300, 800-255-0121. Supplies, books, and beneficial insects.

Gardener's Supply Co., 128 Intervale Road, Burlington, Vermont 05401. Tel.: 802-863-1700. Grower and gardening supplies.

Hobby Growing Supplies, 2242 North Palmer Drive, Schaumberg, Illinois 60173. Tel.: 800-828-2242. Complete horticultural supplies.

Hydroponic Society of America, P.O. Box 6067, Concord, California 94524. Tel.: 510-682-4193.

Mellinger's, 2380AF Range Road, North Lima, Ohio 44452. Free greenhouse brochure.

Plant Collectibles, 103C Kenview, Buffalo, New York 14217. Free catalogue.

Solar Products

Arco Solar, P.O. Box 6032, Camarillo, California 93010. Manufactures solar photovoltaic films.

Atlantic Solar Products, 9351J Philadelphia Road, P.O. Box 70060, Baltimore, Maryland 21237. Tel.: 301-686-2500. Siemens Solar Industries.

Dutchguard, Dept. DP-4, P.O. Box 411687, Kansas City, Missouri 64141. Tel.: 816-221-3581, 800-821-5157. A solar-powered ventilator advertised for cars, but ideal for greenhouses.

Photocomm, Inc., 7681 East Gray Road, Scottsdale, Arizona 85260. Tel.: 602-948-8003, 800-223-9580, extension K. Solar electric systems.

Solar Components Inc., 121 Valley St., Manchester, New Hampshire 03103. Tel.: 603-668-8186; Fax: 603-627-3110. "The largest and oldest solar products catalogue company in the world." A complete 63-page catalogue of solar and energy-saving products for the home owner.

Sunelco, The Sun Electric Company, P.O. Box 1499, Hamilton, Montana 59840. Tel.: 800-338-6844. An 80-page catalogue of information and products.

Information

SOLAR

American Solar Energy Society, 2400 Central Avenue, Unit G1, Boulder, Colorado 80301. Tel.: 303-443-3130. Monthly Magazine—*Solar Today*.

National Renewable Energy Laboratory, 1617 Cole Blvd., Golden, Colorado 80401. Tel.: 303-231-1000.

Solar Energy Industries Association, 777 North Capital St. N.E., Suite 805, Washington, D.C. 2002. Tel.: 703-524-6100. Solar source book.

Solar Times, Sheldon Fredericks Advertising, 655 Washington Blvd., Stanford, Connecticut 06901. Tel.: 203-324-0051; Fax: 203-324-0520.

Sunworld, International Solar Energy Society, Box 8364, Santa Fe, New Mexico 87504. World coverage magazine.

PLANTS AND GROWING

Your nearest botanical garden or arboretum has gardens and greenhouses where you can see all kinds of plants and get information on growing techniques. Addresses are available from the American Association of Botanical Gardens and Arboreta, 786 Church Road, Wayne, Pennsylvania 19087. Tel.: 215-688-1120.

The Avant Gardener, Box 489E, New York, N.Y. 10028. A monthly newsletter. One of the best sources of information on all phases of gardening, including greenhouses.

Gardener's Index, Compudex Press, P.O. Box 27041, Kansas City, Missouri 64110. Annual index to a number of garden magazines.

Hobby Greenhouse Association, 8 Glen Terrace, Bedford, Maine 01730. *Hobby Greenhouse Magazine*.

Source List of Plants and Seeds, Anderson Horticultural Library, Minnesota Landscape Arboretum, 3675 Arboretum Drive, Box 39, Dept. F.G., Chanhassen, Minnesota 55317. Lists 40,000 different plants and 400 mail-order firms in the United States and Canada.

UNITED KINGDOM SOURCES

Home Greenhouse Supplies

Geeco Ltd., New Milton, Hants BH25 6SE. Tel.: 0425-61-4600. Carries the Humex line of greenhouse supplies.

Organic Gardening, Henry Doubleday Research Association, National Centre for Organic Gardening, Ryton-on-Dunsmore, Coventry CV8 3LG. Tel.: 0203-303517. If your interest is organic gardening you should visit the centre and have an organic food meal in the café.

Solar Greenhouse, Serac Ltd., Nyton Road, Aldingbourne, Nr. Chichester, West Sussex P020 6TU. Tel.: 0243-543911. Solar efficiency reduces heating costs by 50%.

Stewart's, The Stewart Bldg., Purley Way, Croydon CR9 4HS. Tel.: 01-686-2231; Fax: 01-688-3857. Planters, pots and supplies.

Two Wests and Elliott, Unit 4, Carwood Road, Sheepbridge Industrial Estate, Chesterfield, Derbyshire S41 9RH. Tel.: 0246-451077. Complete greenhouse and conservatory equipment and supplies and a free catalogue.

Solar Products

Arco Solar Europe Inc., McGraw-Hill House, Shoppenhangers Road, Maidenhead, Berkshire SL6 2QL. Tel.: 0628-75011. Photovoltaic panels, publishes the magazine *Arco Solar News*.

Chronar Ltd., Waterton Industrial Estate, Unit #1, Bridgend, Wales CF31 3YN. Tel.: 0656-61211. Photovoltaic panels, all sizes.

Dulas Engineering Ltd., Llwyngwern Quarry, Machynlleth, Powys, Wales SY20 9AZ. Tel.: 0654-2782. Manufactures the Unitemp air recirculator, which transfers ceiling heat back to the floor.

Low-Energy Supply Systems, 84 Colson St., Bristol BS1 5BB. Tel.: 0272-272530. Small-scale renewable energy equipment.

Northumbrian Energy Workshop Ltd., Acomb, Hexham, Northumberland NE46 4SA. Tel.: 0434-606737. Wind energy systems to power your home solar grower.

The Solar Trade Association, Brackenhurst, Greenham Common South, Newbury RG15 8HH. Tel.: 0635-46561. Fifteen companies specializing in solar technology.

Thermomax Ltd., Balloo Crescent, Bangor, Northern Ireland BT19 2UP. Tel.: 0274-452411. The leaders in the manufacture of evacuated tube solar heating equipment.

Wind and Sun, Laneside House, King's Head Lane, Islip, Oxfordshire OX5 2BZ. Tel.: 08675-6349. Renewable energy.

Information

SOLAR

Appropriate Technology, IT Publications, 9 King St., London WC2E 8HW. Tel.: 01-836-9434. Publishes a monthly journal called *Appropriate Technology*.

Centre for Alternative Technology, Llwyngwern Quarry, Machynlleth, Powys, Wales SY20 9AZ. Tel.: 0654-240. Probably the best source of solar information and products in Britain. Publishes a solar energy resource list of 40 British firms.

PLANTS AND GROWING

There are literally thousands of gardens in Britain where you can get acquainted with plants and their culture. To find out about these gardens contact the Royal Horticultural Society, 80 Vincent Square, London SW1P 2PE.

Dataplant, 25 Malgraves Place, Basildon, Essex SS13 3PY. Tel.: 268-556683. Plant-finding service listing 45,000 plants available in Britain.

The Garden, Home and Law Publishing Ltd., Greater London House, Hampstead Road, London NW1 7QQ. Tel.: 01-388-3171.

Garden Answers (formerly *Greenhouse Magazine*), Park House, 117 Park Road, Peterborough PE1 ZTR. Tel.: 07-33-555161.

The Gardener, Home and Law Publishing Ltd., Greater London House, Hampstead Road, London NW1 7QQ. Tel.: 01-388-3171. Excellent ads for greenhouses and greenhouse supplies.

The Gardeners' Book Society, Brunel House, Newton Abbot, Devon TQ12 2DW. Send for a catalogue.

Hortus, The Neuadd, Rhayader, Powys, Wales LD6 5HH. Articles by distinguished British gardeners.

Practical Gardening, EMAP National Publications Ltd., Bushfield House, Orton Centre, Peterborough PE2 0UW. Tel.: 0733-237111; Fax: 0733-231137. Lots of ads for greenhouses and supplies, and a handy 16-page how-to insert. They also publish *Plants and Gardens*.

INTERNATIONAL

International Solar Energy Society, Institute of Technology, P.O. Box 124, Caulfield East, Victoria, Australia 3145.

Bibliography

BACKGROUND

Butti, Ken and John Perlin. *A Golden Thread: 2500 Years of Solar Architecture and Technology*. New York, N.Y.: Van Nostrand Reinhold, 1980. About 2000 years ago Emperor Tiberius grew cucumbers in a solar greenhouse heat trap!

SOLAR

Anderson, Bruce N. *Ecologue*. New York, N.Y.: Prentice Hall Press, 1990.

Anderson, Bruce and Malcolm Wells. *Passive Solar Energy*. Andover, Massachusetts: Brickhouse Publishing, 1981. Thorough treatment of passive solar. Extensive data in 6 appendices.

Button, John. *The Green Pages*. London, England: Macdonald & Co. A directory of products, services, resources and ideas.

Carter, Joe. *Solarizing Your Present Home*. Emmaus, Pennsylvania: Rodale Press, 1981. A complete coverage of all the ways to use solar energy, including solar greenhouses.

Davis, Norah Deakin and Linda Lindsey. *At Home in the Sun: Open House Tour of Solar Homes in the United States*. Charlotte, Virginia: Garden Way Publishing, 1979.

Derrick, Anthony, Catharine Francis and Varis Bokalders. *Solar Photovoltaic Products*. London, England: Intermediate Technology Publications Ltd., 1991. A buyer's guide with suppliers' addresses.

Elkington, John. *Sun Traps*. New York, N.Y.: Penguin, 1984. Professor Shao Yaun of George Washington University has patented a system for using the earth as a heat storage medium.

The Farallones Institute. *The Integral Urban House*. San Francisco: Sierra Club Books, 1979. Written by a group of architects, engineers and biologists in the San Francisco Bay area. Excellent section on the solar greenhouse.

Knox, Gerald. *Solar Living*. Des Moines, Iowa: Meredith Corporation, 1983. Excellent solar coverage with greenhouse gardening chart.

Nicholson, Nick. *Autonomous House Report*. Ayer's Cliff, Quebec: Ayer's Cliff Centre for Self Sufficiency, 1981. A solar house in cold country! Also wrote *Harvest the Sun*.

Popular Science Magazine. Keeps up-to-date on solar development, both commercial and for the home owner.

Shurcliff, William A. *120 Solar Heated Buildings of North America*. Andover, Massachusetts: Brickhouse Publishing, 1978.

Sunspaces. Chantilly, Virginia: Home Buyer Publications. A guide to more than 100 sunspace manufacturers.

Wild, Russell. *The Earth Care Annual*. Emmaus, Pennsylvania: Rodale Press, 1991. The cost of solar photovoltaic power keeps coming down!

Yanda, William F. and Rick Fisher. *The Food and Heat Producing Solar Greenhouse*. Santa Fe, New Mexico: John Muir Publications, 1980.

PLANTS AND GROWING

Barton, Barbara J. *Gardening by Mail*. Boston: Houghton Mifflin. Lists nearly 500 garden supply companies, 250 garden magazines—an excellent source book for just about everything a gardener needs.

Head, William. *Gardening Under Cover: Northwest Guide to Solar Greenhouses, Cold Frames and Cloches*. Washington: Sasquatch Books, 1989. How to construct coverings for year-round gardening.

Leckie, Jim, Gil Masters, Harry Whitehouse and Lily Young. *More Other Homes and Garbage*. San Francisco, California: Sierra Club Books, 1981. Written by a group from the Stanford School of Engineering. Excellent data on all phases of renewable energy.

Organic Gardening Magazine. Emmaus, Pennsylvania: Rodale Press. One of the oldest and best information sources for the grower. Operates the Rodale Research Center.

Patent, Dorothy Hinshaw and Diane E. Bilderback. *Book of Garden Secrets*. Camden East, Ontario: Camden House Publishing, 1991. A new breed of vegetable garden book that explains how plants function, as well as giving tips on growing techniques.

Wolf, Delores. *Growing Food in Solar Greenhouses*. New York, N,Y.: Doubleday, 1981. Month-by-month guide to growing food in the solar greenhouse.

Of the many garden encyclopedias the following are my favorites for easy reading and excellent coverage:

Hay, Roy and George Elbert. *Practical Gardening Encyclopedia*. New York, N.Y.: Van Nostrand Reinhold, 1977.

Sunset Western Garden Book. 5th ed. Menlo Park, California: Lane Publishing Co., 1988.

Wyman, Donald. *The Gardening Encyclopedia*. New York, N.Y.: Macmillan, 1987.

Index